THE STORY OF DAI A[

For Lollie and Heather

THE STORY OF DAI AILIAN

Icon of Chinese folk dance

Pioneer of Chinese ballet

RICHARD GLASSTONE

DANCE BOOKS

First published in 2007 by Dance Books Ltd
The Old Bakery
4 Lenten Street
Alton
Hampshire GU34 1HG

© 2007 Richard Glasstone

ISBN: 978 1 85273 118 2

A CIP catalogue record for this book is available from the British Library

Printed and bound in Great Britain by Lightning Source

CONTENTS

Resumé   vii
Prologue: Setting the Scene   ix

1. Growing up in Trinidad   1
2. Studying Ballet and Discovering Modern Dance   7
3. Dartington: Love Found and Love Lost   13
4. Hong Kong: China can wait no longer   19
5. Searching for Chinese Folk Dance   23
6. Establishing Classical Ballet in China   44
7. Labanotation in China   54
8. The Cultural Revolution   61
9. Starting Again   71
10. Ballet in China Today   82
11. The problems of choreography in China   89
12. Class with the Chinese Ballet   93

Appendix   96

Index   100

ACKNOWLEDGEMENTS

It would not have been possible for me to write this book without the generous help and co-operation of Madame Dai Ailian. My warmest thanks go to her for her patience and her kindness, and to her assistant Wu Jingshu (Lollie), without whose expert translating I would have been lost.

Mr Clement Crisp kindly read the initial draft of my text and I thank him for his wise comments and for his encouragement.

I am also greatly indebted to Professor Peng Song and Professor Wang Kefen for giving so generously of their time to help me build up a picture of Dai Ailian's pioneering activities of half a century ago.

Mr Cao was enormously welcoming during my visits to the Beijing Dance School where Mr Xu Rui was both my interpreter and my guide. The Artistic Director of the National Ballet of China, Madame Zhao Ruheng, could not have been more helpful and I thank her and her Staff for their invaluable assistance.

In London, Sarah Percival gave me much sound advice regarding publication and my friends Donggao Yang and ShuYongjian helped me translate several Chinese texts. I am grateful to them, and also to family and friends who made it financially possible for me to continue my research in China. Finally, special thanks to my wife, Heather, for continuously urging me to complete the book.

Author's note: The Pinyin system of transliteration of Chinese names and words is now widely used. However, in some texts Dai Ailian's name is spelled Tai Ai-Lian. Her husband's name is variously transliterated as Ye Chien Yu or Ye Qianyu. Such differences in systems of transliteration are the explanation for what might appear to be discrepancies in the spelling of certain names in my text.

Illustrations: With the exception of the photographs of the National Ballet of China which are published courtesy of the Company's Artistic Director, Madame Zhao Ruheng, all the other photographs and drawings are published courtesy of Madame Dai Ailian.

BRIEF RESUME OF MAIN CHAPTER CONTENT

CHAPTER ONE: TRINIDAD. This covers Dai Ailian's childhood. The daughter of an expatriate Chinese family, she was born in Trinidad. The prevailing colonial racial hierarchy there meant that her introduction to ballet came from watching little white English girls through the window of the local dancing school. Finally managing to overcome the existing racial taboo, she joins the class and becomes the star pupil.

CHAPTER TWO: LONDON. Teenaged Dai Ailian studies classical ballet in London with Anton Dolin, Marie Rambert and Margaret Craske. She becomes involved in efforts to aid those people resisting the Japanese invasion of China. Inspired by Edgar Snow's book *Red Star Over China* , she says she '....sees a ray of hope for my suffering motherland'; but her plans to go to China to join the revolution are interrupted by her discovery of Modern Dance. Influenced by Wigman and Jooss, she decides that 'China can wait' and joins Jooss at Dartington.

CHAPTER THREE: DARTINGTON. Greatly influenced by Jooss, Laban and Leeder, Dai's involvment in the artistic life at Dartington eventually leads to a love affair with the sculptor, Willi Soukop. Then the outbreak of the Second World War results in her separation both from her lover and from Jooss, her artistic mentor.

CHAPTER FOUR: HONG KONG. Dai takes part in performances organised by Madame Sun Yat Sen to raise funds to assist the victims of Japanese bombing raids on the Chinese mainland. Then she meets and marries the distinguished Chinese artist, Ye Chien Yu. On the advice of Zhou Enlai, they move to Chongqing where, in spite of constant Japanese air raids, Dai starts teaching and choreographing.

CHAPTER FIVE: RESEARCHING CHINESE FOLK DANCE. Dai journeys through some of the remotest borderlands of China, collecting and recording the little-known dances of the many Minority populations. She stages the first performances of a new form of Chinese dance theatre, choreographing new work inspired by Chinese folk material. With the war over, and the Japanese driven out of China, Dai moves on to Shanghai and Beijing where she becomes the leading figure in the growing revival of interest in the nation's cultural heritage, enthusiastically supported by the new Chinese government. Tours the USA as guest of the State Department, performing Chinese dance.

CHAPTER SIX: ESTABLISHING CLASSICAL BALLET IN CHINA. With the assistance of guest teachers from Soviet Russia, the Chinese government establishes a professional ballet school in Beijing, with Dai as its principal. She goes on to become Artistic Director of the Central Ballet Company which grows out of the school. Following political differences between Mao Zedong and the Soviet Russian government, Russia recalls all its experts from China. Continued political upheaval in China soon leads to the notorious Cultural Revolution.

CHAPTER SEVEN: LABANOTATION IN CHINA. Another of Dai's achievements had been the establishment of the Chinese Labanotation Society. This has played an important role in recording both folk dance and ballet material throughout the country.

CHAPTER EIGHT: THE CULTURAL REVOLUTION. Mao Zedong's decision to banish all Western influence leads to often violent confrontation with artists and intellectuals as the notorious Red Guards embark on the total 're-education' of the population. Dai is among the thousands of artists exiled to the countryside whilst Jiang Qing, Mao's wife, takes over the direction of all artistic life in China.

CHAPTER NINE: STARTING AGAIN. After Mao Zedong's death and the arrest and conviction of his wife and her cronies, life in China gradually returns to some sort of sanity. Dai, now in her new capacity as Artistic Adviser to the National Ballet Company draws on the assistance of her many contacts in the West to help the Chinese dance world to recover its former strengths and, indeed, to surpass them.

CHAPTER TEN: AN OVERVIEW OF BALLET IN CHINA TODAY. A brief look at the development of ballet in Beijing, Shanghai, Guangzhou, Tianjin, Liaoning, and Hong Kong.

APPENDIX: A chronological overview covering all aspects of Dai Ailian's career.

PROLOGUE: SETTING THE SCENE

The Japanese invasion of Manchuria (North East China) in September of 1931 triggered a series of political events worldwide. Within less than a decade these were to lead to the start of the Second World War. The fact that the ominous events of the nineteen thirties were taking place at exactly the same time as the early flowering of ballet in England may seem both irrelevant and somewhat incongruous. Yet it is precisely on that unlikely coincidence that the story of Dai Ailian hinges. The dance-loving daughter of an expatriate Chinese family, Dai Ailian was born in the West Indies, in the British colony of Trinidad. She came to London in the spring of 1931, at the age of fourteen, to study ballet. Her dance studies (initially in classical ballet but later moving to modern dance) dominated the young teenager's day-to-day existence so that, at first, she could have been only dimly aware of the various, increasingly vocal, protest movements springing up in Britain during the nineteen thirties in support of the Chinese resistance to the Japanese invasion of North East China.

Various vested interests in the West (not least those of the British government) were responsible for preventing the League of Nations from taking sufficiently vigorous diplomatic action to stop the Japanese. Meanwhile, in China itself, the Chinese cause was still being hampered by the fierce rivalry between the Kuomintang, the Nationalist party led by Chiang Kaishek, and the Communists led by Mao Zedong. Matters came to a head on the 7th of July 1937, when the Japanese attacked a group of Chinese soldiers near Beijing (the notorious Marco Polo Bridge incident). There had been little significant international opposition to the invasion of North East China in 1931; now the Japanese waited to see how the West would react to this new attack so close to Beijing. After all, further conquest of Chinese territory could well threaten local British and American interests. Yet, within a month, the Japanese felt sufficiently confident to start bombing the strategic port of Tianjin. As a result of this, several British newspapers began warning that Japan's actions were in danger of precipitating a Second World War.

It was against this background that the China Campaign Committee was founded in London in the autumn of 1937. The aim of this committee was to bring together a number of different organisations sympathetic to China's plight. Although the fundamental importance of the China Campaign Committee in helping to co-ordinate action between these various pro-China pressure groups cannot be overstated, we are concerned here primarily with the activities of one particular organisation called Artists International. Founded in London in 1935, this was a group of politically aware artists, actors, writers and musicians who had taken up the Chinese cause. Operating under the auspices of the Campaign Committee, Artists International started staging a series of fund-raising artistic events to help the Chinese. Specifically, the money they raised was used to provide medical assistance for the thousands of victims of the devastating Japanese air raids on Canton and other mainland areas of China. It was through her involvement as a dancer in several of these fund-raising concerts that Dai Ailian was drawn ever closer to the fight for an ancestral homeland which she herself had not yet visited. Indeed, at that time, she still had scant knowledge of Chinese history, culture, or politics and even less of the Chinese language.

The publication, in the autumn of 1937, of Edgar Snow's ground-breaking book *Red Star Over China* was to be the catalyst which finally united the various pro-China pressure groups. Snow's graphic account of the Long March, with his description of the now legendary flight of the Communists from their scattered bases in the South, half-way across China, to the distant Northern city of Yanan, caused a sensation in England. Yanan was the base from which the consolidation of the Chinese Communist Party and the final routing of the Japanese attempt to push from Manchuria to Central China was to be achieved. Snow's book certainly inspired the young Dai Ailian. Her reaction on reading it was 'I seemed to see a ray of hope for my suffering motherland'.

As well as British and other Westerners, Artists International included a number of Chinese members, among them Jack Chen (Chen I Wan), a gifted Shanghai woodcut artist then living in London. It was Jack Chen's sister Sylvia (Chen Si Lan) who, back in Trinidad, had taught the five-year-old Dai Ailian her first tentative dance steps. This had been when the young child took a small part in Sylvia Chen's amateur staging, in 1921, of the musical *Bluebells in Fairyland* (in which Sylvia herself had earlier performed in London). Somewhat incongruously, this turned out to have been the first step on a long trail which, eventually, led Dai Ailian from the London ballet world of the 1930s and her participation in the Artists International fund-raising concerts, via her involvment in the Sino-Japanese war, to her future distinguished position as China's pre-eminent dance specialist – both as a pioneer of classical ballet in China and,

Dai Ailian's grandparents (the boy on the left was her father)

perhaps more importantly, as a dedicated researcher into the rich but little-known traditions of Chinese folk dance.

Fired by the patriotic fervour of the China Campaign Committee and by the concerts organised under its auspices by Artists International – one of these included a famously rousing rendition by the great African American singer Paul Robeson (in Chinese) of the Chinese Army March *The enemy will be silent, China will rise again* – Dai Ailian was to throw in her lot with the thousands now intent on stopping Japan. But before looking into her involvement in the Sino-Japanese conflict, we must retrace our steps to look at Dai's early years in the British colony of Trinidad.

POSTSCRIPT

On February 9th 2006 Dai Ailian died peacefully in hospital in Beijing, happy in the knowledge that I had finished writing her biography and that the manuscript was being prepared for publication.

CHAPTER ONE

GROWING UP IN TRINIDAD

When I first met Dai Ailian she was already eighty years old: a diminutive, exceptionally sprightly figure, leaping up every few minutes to demonstrate some Chinese folk dance step or a ballet exercise remembered from her student days in London, and at the same time rattling off a series of fascinating stories about her amazing life. All this was done with the velocity and the random aim of a machine gun. Indeed she once told me that her loquaciousness had actually earned her the nickname 'machine gun'.

Soon a picture began to emerge of Dai Ailian as a child, growing up in Trinidad: a five-year-old Bluebell in Fairyland improvising a simple dance for the entertainment of her grandmother; an eight-year-old Chinese girl clamouring to be admitted to Miss Walton's ballet lessons for young ladies who, unlike her, were all both white and English; a tiny show-off, later performing Irish and Welsh jigs and a Gypsy number in the dance displays staged by Miss Walton; a bundle of energy, careering around Port of Spain on the new roller skates bought by her devoted father, proud of the attention 'the little Chinese girl' was attracting at these performances.

Then there was also the serious, earnest oriental girl learning to play the piano, studying music from the age of seven to fourteen and successfully passing the Intermediate examination of the Trinity College of Music under a visiting examiner from London; and the eleven-year-old 'pedagogue in embryo' who was to take over the teaching of Miss Walton's ballet pupils when the latter left Trinidad. From an early age, Dai was clearly already that compelling combination of immense energy, vivid imagination, implaccable determination and rare courage who would later go on to survive not only the deprivations and the daily dangers of the Sino-Japanese war, but also the horrors of China's notorious Cultural Revolution, relentlessly pursuing her personal vision of the future of dance in China.

Dai Ailian's grandparents came from the village of Du Ruan, in the Goose Mountain area of Guandong, in the South of China. This is where the *chengzi* oranges ripen out of season without their green skins changing colour, belying the sweetness of the fruit within. Many expatriate Chinese families came originally from the Goose Mountain area which, in the 1950s, became part of Xin Hui. Dai's grandfather was known by his Chinese 'baby name' of Ah Sek or Little Pebble. When he arrived in Trinidad in the late 19th century, the colonial British seemed to find Ah Sek awkward to pronounce, so they took to calling him Isaac. The nick-name stuck; Little Pebble worked hard and the Isaac family prospered. Soon they became wealthy plantation owners and business men, prominent enough to have a local street named after them. To this day there is an Isaac street in the little West Indies town of Couva. Dai Ailian was born in Couva on 10th May 1916. Her father, Dai Yao, was Little Pebble's only son. Aged only eighteen when his father died, Dai Yao inherited the family fortune. Sadly, within a few years, he was to squander most of it on gambling.

Life in twentieth century Trinidad adhered closely to the customary colonial pattern of tacit racial segregation, with the Chinese occupying second place (below the Whites) in the accepted social hierarchy, followed by the Indians and, lastly, the Black population of former slaves. In Port of Spain, where Dai went to school, a favourite Sunday afternoon entertainment was the weekly brass band concert in Government House Gardens. It was as part of the other entertainment on offer at one of these concerts that Dai first saw a demonstration of dancing by a group of English girls, pupils of Miss Nell Walton. The daughter of a local judge, Miss Walton taught ballet once a week but, as was the custom in those days, there were no Chinese children in those classes, much less any Indians or Blacks.

Having discovered that Nell Walton taught at the local Victoria Institute, Dai began watching the ballet classes through the large windows, conveniently kept wide open in the tropical West Indies heat. At the age of five she had enjoyed the very simple dancing Sylvia Chen had taught her for an amateur performance of *Bluebells in Fairyland* but the formal, structured technique of a ballet class was, for Dai, a new and totally fascinating experience. Clearly, Nell Walton must have been a more than competent ballet teacher, because the basic ballet steps Dai was able to imitate from watching and listening through the open windows of the ballet studio were to prove a sound basis for her future professional dance studies.

Dai carefully copied the ballet steps she saw the little English girls performing and then diligently practised all these moves at home. Soon she began begging her mother to let her join Miss Walton's classes. But was that going to be possible for a Chinese child? In those days, this was a potentially delicate matter of social convention; but Nell Walton agreed to consult the pupils' parents. Happily they raised no objections and Dai

Dai Ailian's parents in Trinidad

was allowed to join the classes. To Miss Walton's surprise, Dai had already mastered much of the material just by watching through the open windows and, quite soon, she proved to be one of the most able pupils in the class.

As well as ballet, Miss Walton also taught such dances as Irish and Welsh jigs, the Hornpipe, a Tarantella and one of Dai's favourites, a Gypsy Dance. Before long Dai was performing all of these dances at the regular dance displays staged by Miss Walton and was attracting a good deal of attention from the audiences. The reason she stood out was probably as much due to her genuine, natural dance talent as to her race. 'That's my daughter,' proclaimed the proud Mr Dai Yao. Unusual as it was for a Chinese child to be participating in these English children's recreational activities, it was even more unusual for a Chinese girl to be performing in public in this way. Something that would have been considered unseemly back in China was somehow acceptable for an expatriate Chinese girl living in a British colony.

A dedicated pupil, Dai's dancing improved so rapidly that, when an injury prevented Miss Walton from demonstrating some of the steps in class herself, it was Dai whom she called upon to do so in her place. This seems to have made a favourable impression on the other pupils and on their parents. So much so that, when Miss Walton finally returned to England and the teacher who was to replace her failed to be to the parents' liking, they persuaded Dai to take over the classes. That was how, aged only eleven, Dai Ailian took her first, tentative steps towards a teaching career that would eventually span some sixty years.

As Dai's father gradually gambled away more and more of his inheritance, her mother began to feel the need to equip herself with the means to earn her own living. In 1929 she sailed for Europe where she first studied millinery in France before settling in London, where she worked as a dressmaker. It was from London that she sent her dance-loving daughter a copy of the magazine *The Dancing Times*. Responding to an article in those pages about Anton Dolin and Alicia Markova, Dai wrote to these two ballet stars asking for their photographs. Little did she realise that, before long, she would be studying in London with Dolin himself and that she and Alicia Markova were destined to become life-long friends. Nor could she at that time have had even the faintest inkling of how she was to be drawn into the political protests simmering in England as the Japanese invasion of China gained momentum.

When, shortly after Dai's fifteenth birthday, her mother returned to Trinidad to take her three daughters back to England, Dai wrote to Anton

Dai, standing fourth from the left, with her parents and sisters, Trinidad, circa 1928

Dolin asking him to recommend a ballet school in London. His response was to suggest that, on arrival, she should first join a small group of dancers he was himself coaching privately. So it was that Dai's first ballet lessons in England were to be under the guidance of one of the leading male dancers of the Anglo-Russian ballet world, and in the company of several very promising young dancers. An auspicious start to a dance career that would eventually involve her in an extraordinary Chinese adventure.

CHAPTER TWO

LONDON: STUDYING BALLET AND DISCOVERING MODERN DANCE

In 1931, Anton Dolin (born Patrick Healey-Kay), the handsome Anglo-Irish former young leading male dancer of Diaghilev's prestigious Russian ballet company, was teaching in a small London studio at No. 66 Glebe Place in Chelsea. There was room for only six dancers in these classes: three professional dancers and three teenaged hopefuls. Dai Ailian was one of the latter; another was Wendy Toye. These two youngsters were quite soon to perform together in a famous production of *Hiawatha* at the Albert Hall, Dai's first stage appearance in London. Wendy Toye went on to dance with the Markova-Dolin ballet company prior to embarking on a long and varied career as a choreographer and director of musicals and pantomimes. Of the adult dancers in the class, the young ballerina, Alicia Markova, was a superb role model for young Dai, as well as becoming one of her closest friends. Dai also struck up a friendship with the third of the teenagers in the group, Birgitta Hartwig. Birgitta later adopted the stage name of Vera Zorina when she danced for George Balanchine, the future ballet master and choreographer of the New York City Ballet, whom she was to marry. It was Birgitta's mother who soon encouraged Dai to join her daughter in attending additional ballet classes with Marie Rambert.

Marie Rambert's tiny Mercury Theatre in Notting Hill Gate was where the Ballet Club, cradle of the fledgling English ballet, performed on Sunday nights. Here Dai came into contact with the future famous names of ballet in England: artists such as the young choreographers, Frederick Ashton and Antony Tudor; dancers like Maude Lloyd and Prudence Hyman who were creating important roles in early Tudor and Ashton ballets, as well as the stage designer and dancer William Chappell. This was an exciting and eventful period in the early days of British ballet, following the death in 1929 of the great Russian impressario Serge Diaghilev, whose Ballet Russe company had dominated the Western dance world for most of the past twenty years.

In parallel with Marie Rambert's Ballet Club, the young Ninette de Valois was beginning to establish the Sadler's Wells Ballet (later to become Britain's Royal Ballet Company). Being plunged into the hothouse of creative energy that was London's ballet world of the 1930s was to have a formative and far-reaching effect on the young Dai Ailian. Her remarkable understanding of the art of ballet in general and choreography in particular was forged in that intensely stimulating environment. Dai Ailian's sensitive understanding of the finer points of the art of choreography has earned her the admiration and respect of her colleagues in the West; that her views on this subject are not now always equally appreciated in China itself is a matter of some regret.

Dai Ailian's sound and detailed understanding of the teaching of classical ballet technique was acquired through her studies with the third and the most important of her London teachers, Margaret Craske. Craske was the foremost disciple of one of the greatest ballet pedagogues of his generation, Maestro Enrico Cecchetti. This Italian virtuoso dancer had migrated to Russia in the late 19th century, where he coached many of the young stars of the Imperial Russian Ballet (such as Anna Pavlova and Vaslav Nijinsky) before opening his London studio. Here, during the 1920s, many of the émigré Russian dancers and the new generation of English dancers came to study with Maestro Cecchetti. When he retired to Italy in 1928, Cecchetti handed over his London studio to Margaret Craske.

When Dai Ailian started attending Margaret Craske's classes she again found herself working in the company of the cream of London's dance talent. It was Craske who initiated Dai into the fundamentals of Cecchetti's remarkable teaching theories. The principles underlying Cecchetti's method of training were to underpin Dai's own teaching for more than sixty years. Commenting on the effect Craske's classes had on her, Dai Ailian said that 'They made me feel so light. I felt I was walking on clouds as I left her lessons. I've never had that feeling from other teachers' classes.' Based on the sound principles of Cecchetti's teaching method '....Craske's classes were so scientifically structured that they made me feel that my body was totally liberated.'

In the mid-1930s, several of the former ballerinas from Diaghilev's now defunct Ballet Russe company were living in London. One of them was Lydia Sokolova. Born Hilda Munnings, she was actually English, but it was fashionable at that time for English dancers to adopt Russian stage names. It was Sokolova who taught Dai Ailian the Prelude and the Waltz from Fokine's famous ballet, *Les Sylphides*, a moonlit evocation of the Romantic period, set to a series of Chopin piano pieces. No one could have imagined that, within a few years, Dai was going to be performing these

Dai performing in London, in the mid-thirties, at a fund-raising concert for victims of the Japanese invasion

ephemeral dances in China in the remote, war-torn province of Sichuan, as the Red Army was struggling to repulse the Japanese invaders.

These extracts from *Les Sylphides* were indeed later added to a programme Dai Ailian staged in China and made up in part of dances she had choreographed herself during her stay in London. In preparing her performances for the Artists International fund-raising concerts in London in the mid-thirties, Dai had been greatly helped by the distinguished piano teacher George Woodhouse who, together with the Kahl family, had taken the young Chinese dancer under their wing. Dorothy, the elder of the Kahl daughters, who had studied art, took Dai to museums and exhibitions of painting. She also designed and made the costumes for Dai's dance recitals. The younger Kahl daughter, Peggy, who was studying music with Dai's mentor, George Woodhouse, would accompany Dai's dances on the piano. She also introduced Dai to Woodhouse's assistant, Elizabeth Mason, with whom Dai now continued her own piano studies.

Professor Woodhouse himself took a personal interest in Dai Ailian's early attempts at choreography, guiding her in matters of musical taste. It was also he who pushed her to start performing in public, telling her quite bluntly 'My dear, you must get a job.' 'But I can't get into a ballet company,' Dai protested, 'I'm the wrong height and the wrong colour.' The fact that she was only four foot something tall had indeed been used as the reason for turning her down at several ballet auditions: clearly a convenient way of avoiding the issue of her race in a ballet environment that was still exclusively white. Woodhouse retorted, 'Never mind that; you must get people to see you dance. Get a job anywhere, even in cabaret. Just so long as there's an audience to see you perform.' Dai took his advice and secured an engagement dancing for the diners at the Savoy hotel. Professor Woodhouse continued to vet Dai's choice of music for her choreography and, together with the Kahl sisters and Betty Mason, these good friends gave Dai what she has described as, 'the practical basis of my artistic education.'

By the late 1930s, with her father bankrupted by mounting gambling debts and her mother now seriously ill, Dai Ailian was having to fend for herself. She was able to make a little money by posing as a model at the Slade School of Art and was also involved in some of the first dances created as part of the earliest experiments in British television. For these, and for the fund-raising Artists International performances, she had now started to choreograph dances based on Chinese themes. Although, at that time, she had never seen any authentic Chinese dance, she was inspired by reading about Chinese history and culture in the British Museum library. Also influenced by her growing awareness of the plight of the Chinese people under Japanese occupation, she started to choreograph dances symbolic of the poverty and the oppression of the Chinese peasants, notably a dance accompanied only by the sound of chopsticks tapping against an empty rice bowl.

Through her growing involvement with the China Campaign Committee and the China Institute, Dai Ailian was increasingly coming into contact with people from mainland China and was finding herself drawn more and more to the idea of travelling to her ancestral homeland. But a different departure in dance was starting to attract her attention and was soon to open a new chapter in both her professional and her private life. This was her discovery of modern dance. It was also during the 1930s that the work of several German expressionist modern dancers had started to be seen in London, among them the extraordinarily dramatic Mary Wigman. 'Her way of dancing was so individual, so personal, it was not something one could begin to imitate. But she opened my eyes to the wider possibilities of the art of theatre dance.'

Eager to learn more about the new school of German modern dance, Dai now joined the classes of Lesley Burrows-Goossens, one of the few modern dance exponents then teaching in London, a city still far more attuned to the traditional, more escapist world of classical ballet. Fascinated by the different, much more intellectual approach of these modern dance enthusiasts, Dai began experimenting with some of their ideas.The adherents of the German expressionist dance movement (in parallel with the early pioneers of American modern dance, such as Martha Graham) were intent on devising new ways of dancing, totally removed from the aesthetics and the formalised dance technique of traditional classical ballet. Intrigued by the theories of the modern dance exponents but also very conscious of the limitations of their technical vocabulary, Dai tried to persuade Lesley Burrows-Goossens to draw on some elements of the classical ballet movement vocabulary, adapting it to the new expressionist approach. To a purist like Burrows-Goossens this was anathema. Unlike the situation in today's dance world, where the boundaries between ballet and modern dance have become increasingly blurred, in the 1930s the followers of classical ballet and the pioneers of modern dance still formed two, distinct opposing factions, constantly at loggerheads with one another. So Dai's ideas were seen as treacherous to the modernist cause and she was asked rather unceremoniously to leave the Burrows-Goossens school. There followed a period performing (unpaid) with Ernst and Lotte Berk, two of the so-called 'barefoot dancers' of the German expressionist school. For one of their shows Dai had to learn to make masks. Ever resourceful, she was soon able to turn this newly-acquired skill into another means of making a little money to support herself.

It was at about this time that Betty Mason invited Dai Ailian to accompany her to a performance of the Ballets Jooss. At first Dai was reluctant to accept this invitation. 'I know all the ballet tricks,' was her initial reaction. Enthused as she was by now with the innovative work of Wigman, Ernst and Lotte Berk and Lesley Burrows-Goossens, Dai had become a little disillusioned with ballet. 'Compared to the other arts, such as painting, music and literature, I was beginning to feel that there was something lacking in ballet. It seemed to be more of an entertainment than a serious art form.' Hence Dai's initially unenthusiastic reaction to Betty Mason's invitation to a Ballets Jooss performance. What Dai had not yet realised was that this was not a traditional ballet company, but one of the most innovative and serious dance groups of the day.

Indeed, Kurt Jooss was the first choreographer of international renown to achieve a successful synthesis of classical and modern dance elements to express topical, contemporary ideas in a strikingly theatrical manner. His choreography, free as it was from all artificial convention, was exactly what Dai had been searching for. His masterpiece, *The Green Table*, which depicts the machinations of politicians and the horrors of war as they affect ordinary people (and which had won a prestigious prize for choreography in 1932) made such an impression on Dai Ailian that she decided to shelve her evolving plans to travel to China, in the hope that she might be able to work with Kurt Jooss who, having recently fled Nazi Germany, was now working in England. 'This was what I had been searching for,' she declared, 'China can wait.'

CHAPTER THREE

DARTINGTON: LOVE FOUND AND LOVE LOST

Dartington Hall, part of an ancient mediaeval estate in Devon, was bought in 1925 by Leonard and Dorothy Elmhirst and was renovated by them with the goal of introducing progressive education into what was at that time a depressed rural economy. In 1935, the Dartington Hall Trust, a registered charity, was set up to run the estate as a conference centre and a venue for a variety of artistic activities and social experiments.

As Hitler and the Nazis tightened their grip on 1930s Germany, Kurt Jooss was one of a number of artists and intellectuals who fled to England. Prior to this, Jooss had been one of the leading figures in the German modern dance movement, directing the dance department of the famous Folkwang School in Essen and choreographing many important dance works for his company, the Folkwang Tanzbuhne. The most influential of these was *The Green Table*, a prescient choreographic depiction of the horrors of war engendered by the sterile, self-interested debates of politicians. This production was to become the trade-mark of Jooss' dance group, now re-named the Ballets Jooss when, in 1933, they had to leave Germany. Jooss was offered a residency at Dartington Hall which now became the base for both his school and his company.

Soon after Dai Ailian had seen the Ballets Jooss performing in London she had attended an open audition for the company. Although Jooss did not engage her as a dancer, he clearly thought highly enough of her potential to offer Dai a full scholarship to study with him at Dartington. This proved to be the start of a short but immensely influential chapter in Dai Ailian's development, both as an artist and as a young woman.

As well as working with Jooss, Dai also studied with his close Folkwang colleague, now his main assistant at Dartington, Sigurd Leeder. Like Jooss, Leeder was also a disciple of Rudolf von Laban, the 'high priest' of the Central European school of modern dance.

Laban's whole life had been devoted to researching, analysing and recording both the theory and the practice of harmonious movement, as opposed to conventional step-based dancing. The basic vocabulary of classical ballet is derived largely from two main sources: European folk dance and European court dance, the latter being in many ways a more refined development of the former. All three – ballet, court and folk dance – are essentially based on a vocabulary of steps, be it the simple steps of folk dancing, the more refined steps of aristocratic court dance, or the complex, highly stylised and technically demanding steps of classical ballet. One of the fundamental differences between all these step-based ways of dancing and the type of modern dance pioneered by Rudolf von Laban is that he envisaged dance not in terms of steps but as what he described as 'the flow of movement pervading all articulations of the body'.

One of Laban's most practical achievements was his development of a highly detailed system of movement notation, first published in the late 1920s under the title *Kinetographie* and later developed into what is now called Labanotation. As part of her studies with Jooss and Leeder at Dartington, Dai Ailian was introduced to Laban's space-movement theories in general and to his system of movement notation in particular. Laban's theories were to have a major impact on Dai's artistic development and her admiration for his work soon began to equal her devotion to the teachings of the ballet pedagogue, Enrico Cecchetti. The Chinese use two separate words to differentiate between a paternal and a maternal grandfather: Dai Ailian came to regard Cecchetti as her spiritual 'Ye Ye' or 'Zu Fu' (her 'paternal grandfather') and Laban as her 'maternal spiritual ancestor' her 'Lao Ye' or 'Wai Zu Fu'.

If her studies with Jooss and Leeder had a far-reaching effect on Dai's development as a dancer, and later as a teacher and choreographer, there was another and a no less important encounter awaiting her at Dartington in the person of Willi Soukop. One of several distinguished artists working at Dartington (including the painter Hein Heckroth and the potter Bernard Leach), Willi Soukop was a hugely talented young sculptor. Wilhelm Josef Soukop was born in Vienna on 5th January 1907. His father Karl, a Czecheslovakian shoemaker who never overcame the horrors he had witnessed in the trenches during the First World War, had committed suicide. Twelve-year-old Willi had had to support the family by carving hundreds of umbrella handles in a factory by day while also attending evening classes at Vienna's Academy of Fine Art, where he learnt to appreciate both Classical and Expressionist Art. The Dartington School Administrator, Kay Star, during a trip to Vienna in 1935, had seen Soukop's work and invited him to visit England.

Dai Ailian's initial scholarship to Dartington Hall had been for the six-week period of the Summer School. Jooss now offered her a second scholarship to his school. But whereas during the Summer School all her living expenses were taken care of, there was now a period of two weeks before the start of the new term during which Dai was going to have to

Willi Soukop at Dartington *Photo: courtesy of Michael Soukop*

Dai Ailian in 1993 with the sculpted portrait Willi Soukop made of her in 1939 at Dartington *Photo: Martin Mayer, courtesy of the RAD*

fend for herself. She had formed a friendship with Hein Heckroth, the designer of *The Green Table*, who used to lend her one of his paintings each week to hang in her room. Initially, it had been agreed that Dai would pose for Heckroth in return for him meeting her living expenses during that two-week break before the start of the new course. However, once the war had started Heckroth, a Jewish refugee from Nazi Germany, became too depressed to continue working. Willi Soukop would also have liked to have Dai pose for him but, like her, he too had very little money. Ever resourceful, Dai made Willi the following offer: 'If you will give me the money you would normally be spending on your meals in the White Hart dining room, I will use it to cook for you and there will be enough to eat for both of us.' Which was how Dai Ailian came to live with Willi Soukop, cooking his meals, mending his clothes, and falling head over heels in love with him.

The beautiful sculptured head Soukop made of Dai at this time was exhibited at the Royal Academy of Arts in London in the early 1950s; another is housed at London's Royal Academy of Dancing and there is also one in the Dance Museum in Stockholm. Dai was certainly a source of great inspiration to this fine young sculptor and her admiration for his work, coupled with her deep affection for him as a man, forged a special bond between them that was to survive many vicissitudes and last a lifetime. Sadly, as was the case with so many young people, the war intervened to disrupt personal relationships as well as career plans. The school at Dartington had to close and Dai was forced to move on. Willi Soukop, who had previously been engaged to marry one of Dai's classmates, Simone Moser, had become temporarily separated from his fiancée who was stuck in Paris, as well as from his own family in Vienna. As an Austrian citizen, he was regarded as an enemy-alien and in 1940 he was interned for several months. Meanwhile Dai, unable to find work as a dancer, was once again contemplating trying to get to China.

Willi did eventually marry Simone Moser. Dai's destiny was finally going to take her to her ancestral homeland. It would be many years before she and Willi were to meet again. Yet, in spite of her two marriages during her time in China, the love that had blossomed between Dai and Willi during those penniless but blissfully happy weeks at Dartington never faded. Eventually, Dai was able to return to the West and to renew her friendship with both Willi and Simone. After the war Soukop had settled in London. His work gradually gained wider recognition and, in 1963, he became an Associate of the Royal Academy of Arts, and a full Academician six years later. His deep understanding of craftsmanship

Dai at about the
time she met
Willi Soukop at
Dartington

and his openess of stylistic approach made him a much sought-after teacher as well as a distinguished sculptor in his own right. Exactly forty-nine years after first meeting at Dartington,and following the death of Simone, Dai was to nurse the ailing Soukop through the final days preceding his death in 1995. But in between their first assignation and their final parting, Dai Ailian had her epic Chinese adventure to live out.

CHAPTER FOUR

HONG KONG: CHINA CAN WAIT NO LONGER

When Kurt Jooss had offered Dai Ailian a scholarship to study with him at his Dartington Summer School, she had grasped the opportunity. 'China can wait!' she had exclaimed, shelving her developing plans to try to travel there. Now, with the whole of Europe plunged into war and her beloved Dartington Hall closed down, the time seemed right at last to realise her dream to explore her ancestral homeland.

Although she had never been to China, Dai's awareness of her Chinese roots had been strengthened through her involvement with London's China Campaign Committee and the Artists International's fund-raising concerts in aid of the victims of the Sino-Japanese conflict. Reading Edgar Snow's compelling account of the Red Army's progress in his book *Red Star Over China* may well have been the actual catalyst which convinced Dai that China was where her destiny lay. Yet, somewhere beneath the surface, she had long been subliminally aware of that destiny. 'When I was a student in London and even before that, back in Trinidad, we were always aware that we were Chinese and that even though we had been born abroad, in an expatriate family, China was our true homeland.'

'In those early days, we expatriate Chinese youngsters knew more about Hong Kong and Canton than about the rest of the country, which we used to refer to as "North China". To us, that was a distant, intriguing and somewhat mysterious land; but although we knew little about it, we were always very conscious of the fact that it was where we belonged. When I arrived in London, I met other Overseas Chinese from Singapore and Malaysia and even one boy from Australia, also studying in England. But there were also other students who came from mainland China, from Shanghai and Tianjin and Beijing and they could all speak Chinese, which I couldn't! I used to go to the British Museum Library to read about Chinese history. From my reading I realised that ours was a great culture which, like other Asian cultures, must surely have included a dance tradition. Yet, although I had seen performances of Japanese, Indian and Javanese dance in London, I was unable to find any Chinese dance.'

Thanks to a number of social activities organised by London's very active China Institute, Dai gradually came into contact with increasing numbers of people from mainland China. 'I thought they were superior to Overseas Chinese like me, because they understood the culture and they could speak the language. I envied them so much! I knew in my heart that, some day, I must go to China.' Now, with Dartington Hall closed and her beloved Willi Soukop interned as an enemy alien, that day had come for Dai Ailian.

Previous attempts to raise the money for the fare, or to find a way to work her passage to China had all come to nought. At last, help was at hand in the person of Zhang Su Li, the curator at London's Chinese Institute, who also happened to be on the committee tasked with administering a special fund intended for the repatriation of needy Chinese students living in England. He was well aware of, and sympathetic to Dai's ambition to travel to China to find her roots and to rediscover Chinese dance. So, somehow, he found a way of drawing on that repatriation fund to finance Dai's passage. He knew that she had an aunt living in Hong Kong and, in any case, that was where he advised her to go to begin with, rather than attempting to travel directly to mainland China which, of course, was her ultimate goal.

Thanks to Zhang Su Li's intervention, finally, in January of 1940, Dai Ailian was able to board a ship of the Blue Funnel Line at Liverpool, bound for Hong Kong. The journey was to take seven weeks. The weather was freezing; several of the passengers became quite seriously ill and the ship's cook died and had to be buried at sea. But at last Dai's dream of travelling to China was coming true. Soon after her arrival in Hong Kong, and once she had recovered from the bronchitis contracted during the long and miserably cold sea voyage, Dai Ailian was invited to a meeting with Madame Sun Yat Sen (Song Quingling), the widow of the founder of the first Chinese Republic. Since her husband's death in 1925, she had fought to preserve his legacy in the face of the acute factionalism which was dividing the country.

During the Sino-Japanese war Madame Sun Yat Sen's China Defence League also administered the funds raised in England and America by the Chinese Campaign Committee, for the medical aid of the victims of the anti-Japanese war. As we have seen, Dai Ailian had performed regularly at those fund-raising concerts and Madame Sun Yat Sen was well aware of the success she had enjoyed. Now she invited her to perform at a similar event in Hong Kong, sharing the stage with the singer Shi Yi Qui. Their performance was enthusiastically received and raised a considerable amount of money, as well as resulting in an even greater general awareness of the anti-Japanese resistance movement's activities. This prompted Madame Sun Yat Sen to persuade Dai to delay her planned departure to the interior of the Chinese mainland in order to perform again at a second fund-raising event. 'When I agreed to do this, little did I realise that there was going to be a delay of some eleven months before that second concert took place. Money was short but luckily my sister who was living in Penang was able to help a little. As it turned out, that long delay in Hong Kong was to have some unexpectedly happy consequences for me.'

As Dai was preparing some new dances for this second fund-raising performance, rehearsing on the only available space, the slippery floor of a Hong Kong ballroom, she agreed – somewhat reluctantly – to a request from some Chinese artists to be allowed to sketch her during her rehearsal. 'I agreed to this, but I also made it clear that I would not interrupt my rehearsal in order to pose for them: they would just have to sketch me as I worked. When I had finished my rehearsal, I decided to have a look at what they had managed to draw. I was amazed at the beautiful sketches of me by one of the assembled artists. Looking at him, I saw that he was handsome; his drawings of me were wonderful; and suddenly I began to think that I could fall in love with such a man and forget Willi Soukop.'

Within just two weeks, Dai was engaged to Ye Chien Yu who, as she had by then discovered, was already a famous illustrator and cartoonist from Zhe Jiang, divorced, with two young children. In January of 1941, almost a year from when she had arrived in China, Dai and Ye Chien Yu (now often transliterated as Ye Qianyu) were married.

Before long they would be embarking on the long journey into the interior. At first Dai had planned to travel to Yanan, in the so-called 'liberated area' of China; but Zhou Enlai, (to whom she had a letter of introduction from Madame Sun Yat Sen) advised against this. 'For one thing, you don't yet speak Chinese very well', he told her 'and in any case your particular talents will be of more use to the people in Chongqing.' He was proved right, for it was indeed to be in Chongqing and later in Chengdu, that Dai Ailian's re-discovery of China's great dance heritage was to begin.

The journey into the interior was long and arduous. Dai and her husband had first to travel by boat to Macau, before accessing the mainland. From Guangzhou they had to proceed in stages, by bus and truck and even partly by bicycle or on foot, until an ancient, clapped-out bus finally deposited them in Chongqing. Here, at last, was the real China.

Dai and her husband, the artist Ye Chien Yu, in 1942

CHAPTER FIVE

SEARCHING FOR CHINESE FOLK DANCE FROM CHONGQING TO CHENGDU AND SHANGHAI TO BEIJING

Chongqing is the most important industrial city in Sichuan province. Surrounded by mountains, this vast, fertile region of China, known as 'heaven's granary', derives its name from the Chinese for four streams – *si chuan* – the four tributaries feeding the mighty Yangtze river bordering Tibet. Chongqing was the city where Chiang Kaishek, China's Nationalist (Kuomintang) leader, had established his war-time capital during the Japanese invasion and the Chinese Civil War. Although forced to co-operate temporarily with the Communist leader, Mao Zedong, against the Japanese, Chiang Kaishek's true ambition was eventually to wipe out the Communists – even if this meant ceding some territory to Japan.

By the time of Dai Ailian's arrival, the Japanese invasion had already led to vast numbers of refugees from all over China fleeing to Chongqing. Although the Japanese subjected the city to repeated, merciless bombing raids, they never did manage to capture Chongqing. Cultural activities continued to flourish in spite of the bombing, no doubt partly boosted by the number of refugee artists and musicians swelling the local population. This then was where Dai (together with her husband, the artist Ye Chien Yu) was to spend the five years from 1941 to 1945.

However, within a few months of arriving in Chongqing, Dai had to interrupt the dance teaching and performing she had started there in order to return to Hong Kong for an emergency surgical operation. Sadly, this was to result in Dai being unable to have any children of her own, although she was later to prove to be a caring step-mother to the young daughter from her husband's first marriage. It was whilst she was convalescing in Hong Kong after that major operation that Dai and her husband – who had now joined her there – were to become involved in a dramatic and potentially perilous adventure.

'It was Christmas day. We had gone out for a walk when I heard the distant sound of what I immediately recognized as Japanese aircraft. It was a sound I had already become all too familiar with from the Japanese air raids in Chongqing. Anticipating what was to be the imminent

Japanese invasion of Hong Kong, we fled the city, making for the surrounding mountainous territory, with only the clothes we were wearing, and abandoning passports, documents and all our personal possessions. That night, as we struggled to find our way in the dark, I stumbled and fell into a pile of manure. Luckily, we managed to find a stream where I was able to wash myself and get rid of some of the stink. Exhausted, we fell asleep out there, in the open. Next morning we awoke to find the local villagers had brought us some food – rice and dog meat – as well as a blanket. Although we were starving, I couldn't bring myself to eat the dog meat; but that blanket was a godsend: we took it in turns to wrap ourselves in it as we undressed and each washed our only set of clothing.'

In the following few days, Dai and her husband were more than once caught up in the cross-fire between the invading Japanese and the remnants of the British still trying to defend the colony. 'We fled further and further into the hills, pursued by Japanese soldiers searching for food. We hid in the woods by day, emerging by night to sleep in the relative safety of some friendly farmhouse. The one unexpectedly lucky aspect of our ordeal was that the local farmers, rather than let the Japanese requisition their livestock, decided to slaughter their animals, inviting us to join in nightly feasts of pork and chicken – better food than we had had in war-torn Chongqing or even in Hong Kong.'

It was to be many weeks, and only after a number of close escapes from the marauding Japanese that, ill and exhausted, Dai and her husband were eventually able to make their way back to Chongqing where the astonishingly resilient population, in defiance of the increasing Japanese threat, were resolutely continuing with their day to day lives, pursuing their recreational and cultural activities. Dai started teaching dance again, at the National Opera School and the National Institute for Social Education. Several of the young adults she taught there were later themselves to become dance teachers. Soon to join them was a young man called Peng Song.

A drama student as well as a fine musician Peng, already in his late twenties, had had only a minimal amount of previous dance training. Having read newspaper accounts of Dai's arrival from England and of the success of her Hong Kong dance recitals, Peng asked Dai if he could study with her. Initially reluctant to take him on because of his age, but thinking his musical and dramatic expertise could well be an asset in the small performing group she had started to assemble, Dai accepted Peng as a dance student. Her initial doubts about him were soon dispelled: this highly intelligent and gifted young man was destined not only to become Dai's dance partner as well as a fine teacher but, later on, a distinguished and highly respected Professor of Dance History at the Beijing Dance Academy.

In April 2005, I had the honour of meeting Professor Peng in Beijing. He was a tall, dignified gentleman in his late eighties. He talked to me at length about those early days with Dai in Chongqing. He recalled that his initial reaction on reading newspaper accounts of Dai's arrival from England was, 'Why would an artist like her decide to come to China at such a difficult time, with half the country occupied by enemy forces? I wondered how she would survive the harsh war-time conditions? We had no money and very little food. No rice, just congee and soya beans; and the Japanese were bombing us almost daily.' Going on to describe her performances, the Professor grew more and more animated as he related what had clearly been one of the formative experiences of his youth.

'To see Dai Ailian dance her solo *Longing for Home* was something intensely moving. The music for this dance had been composed by the famous violinist, Ma Si Chong. Like so many of us, he too had fled to Chongqing to escape the Japanese. Dai's sensitive choreographic interpretation of Ma's music made a deep impression on everyone present. We were watching Dai dance but our thoughts were of the homes we had had to abandon. After Dai's performance there was dead silence for several minutes before the audience burst into applause.'

Another of Dai's dances was called *Sale*. It told the story of two children whose parents were forced to sell them into possible slavery so as to save the rest of the family from starvation. 'Today, that may sound melodramatic to you,' said Peng ' but it was a true reflection of the desperate conditions some families had been reduced to in the course of China's tragic history.' Professor Peng then described Dai's choreography for a piece called *Air Raid*. This was about a mother disturbed by the ghost of her dead daughter, killed by a Japanese bomb. Peng Song and his classmate, Long Zheng Qiu, (Dai's first two male students) were to perform the roles of the distraught mother's two sons. He recalled how the first performance had had to be postponed for two weeks out of respect for the carnage caused when a huge Japanese bomb scored a direct hit on Chongqing's main air-raid shelter, killing everyone inside. Quietly and with immense dignity, Peng told me that '... it took eight huge trucks for us to clear away all those bodies'.

As Professor Peng related these personal experiences going back some sixty years, it became clear to me that what had inspired him most about

Drawing by Ye Chien Yu of Dai in her solo 'Longing for Home'

Dai's choreography was the fact that, as he put it: 'her work was about humanity, not just entertainment. You were watching one picture on stage, but seeing many other pictures in your head.' Suddenly I saw the connection with what Dai had told me about her experience of seeing Kurt Jooss' *The Green Table* in London in the late 1930s. Jooss' simple but devastating depiction of the horrors of war and the machinations of war-mongering politicians in *The Green Table* had so deeply impressed her that she had shelved her early plans to travel to China so as to be able to go to study with Jooss at Dartington. His influence on her subsequent work was clear to see. Like Jooss, her dance vocabulary was rooted in the basics of ballet technique, but enriched through her experience of Central European modern dance and informed by the grim realities of life in a war zone.

A remarkable feature of 1940s Chongqing was the Yu Cai school for talented children, many of them orphans, run by the internationally renowned educationalist, Tao Xin Zhi. His progressive teaching methods encouraged a 'hands on' approach; according to individual ability, his pupils were taught music, singing, painting, dancing and drama. In 1944, Tao appointed Dai as Teacher and Head of the Dance Section of the Yu Cai school. Her work there was to have a beneficial and far-reaching influence on the future careers of many young Chinese artists.

Soon Dai began to feel the need to learn more about traditional Chinese dance, in particular that of China's Ethnic Minority Peoples, living in semi-autonomous regions along the so-called 'Chinese Borderlands'. In this she was strongly supported by Tao Xin Zhi, who organised a benefit performance to send Dai to the remote mountain area of Sichuan province. Dai and her husband now set off into the interior, accompanied by Peng Song, whose job it would be to notate the music for the dances Dai was hoping to learn from the Khampas Tibetans.

They got as far as Chengdu, the capital of Sichuan province, where they were to await the arrival of the man who was to be their guide. Because he traded with Tibet, India and China, he knew the difficult terrain that lay ahead – but they were to have to wait three months for him to arrive. During this time, the money started to run out. Then news of the Japanese surrender reached them and Dai's husband wanted to abandon their expedition and move on to Shanghai, China's sophisticated artistic centre. But Dai was determined to carry on. Their guide finally arrived to lead them on their slow, tortuous journey, first by bus, then on foot along a dried out river bed and across a rickety, makeshift bridge, deep into the mountainous region of Xikang, home of the militant Khampas people from eastern Tibet. This was where, finally, Dai was able to learn the little-known Batang Xuanzi dances which she was later to record in Labanotation, thus preserving these ancient dances for posterity.

Meanwhile, it was agreed that Peng Song should undertake some research of his own in some of the other nearby but even more difficult to reach Minority Areas. This is how he described that adventure to me. 'The Yi people, whose area I had wanted to explore, still practised slavery. I was warned that there was a real danger of my being captured by slave-traders unless I was guaranteed safe passage by one particularly influential man. After trying to track him down for nearly a month, a different opportunity arose. This was to explore the area of the Qiang people. Accompanied by a local university student also interested in ethnographical research, I set off into the mountains.'

'There were no roads. For four days we walked along the Ming Jiang river bed. There were no trees, no birds, no people. Unable to find the village we were looking for, I became separated from my companion just as the sun was setting. The steep mountain range further ahead looked like undulating waves in the sea of rapidly encroaching darkness. I was lost, lonely and afraid. I thought I glimpsed some movement in the dark. Was it a human being? No, it was a cat. If there was a cat there must be people. There was hope! I followed the cat. Suddenly I came across the first signs of human habitation.'

What Professor Peng now proceeded to describe were some strange, tall structures serving both as ramparts guarding the area and as living quarters for individual families. He had finally stumbled on a true Qiang mountain settlement. The Qiang nationality are descended from one of China's most ancient peoples, the Xia dynasty. In ancient times, Xia Emperor Da Yu lived near the Jia Shan and the mountain settlement for which Peng had been searching. Because of widespread intermarriage with the Zhou dynasty, there are now very few pure ethnic Qiang people to be found.

Entering the settlement, Peng came across the inhabitants gathered around a fountain in the centre of the village. They made no attempt either to speak or to make eye contact with him until their head man arrived, the only one who could speak a little Mandarin. 'I've come to learn your music and your dances,' said Peng. The head man looked surprised, but he welcomed Peng warmly. He took him along to a dilapidated school room where he indicated that Peng could spread his bedding on top of the school desks. An old nun from a nearby temple lit a lamp for him. 'That nun was an excellent drummer. Never before had I heard such wonderfully complex drumming.'

The next day, some young men showed Peng their homes. They sang songs for him and he notated the melodies. Peng soon realised that the head man was a shaman because he told him that '... our dances chase away the ghosts at funerals'. He later showed him the ritual in which two shamans sing and dance at funerals, one of them wielding a stick decorated with three strips of differently coloured cloth, the other beating a drum made from lamb skin. A mock battle ensues, in which the two shamans and the ghost of the deceased chase each other around until the shamans finally manage to get rid of the ghost. Based on this remarkable experience, Peng Song later choreographed a dance called *Duan Gung* (Shaman Chasing Away Ghosts).

Peng also travelled to the area of the Jia Rong, a branch of the Tibetan people. From them he learnt a drinking song which the villagers sing as they dance around a large wine jar, drinking wine through bamboo straws. He taught both this dance and the shaman dance to Dai Ailian to add to her steadily increasing repertoire of traditional Minority folk dances. Some of these she learnt from the various Cultural Minorities who happened to be working in Sichuan province at that time, including notably a group of Uyghurs from Xinjiang.

By 1946, Dai Ailian had collected enough material to enable her to mount, for the first time in China, a full programme inspired by the traditional folk dances of Cultural Minority populations. This historic performance, staged in Chongqing under the title 'Borderlands Music and Dance', included dances and songs from the Uyghurs, Qiang, Tibetans, Yi and Jia Rong peoples: a triumphant realisation of Dai's long-held ambition to celebrate the folklore of her ancestral homeland.

One of the most popular items on the many different dance programmes Dai Ailian staged in the mid-1940s in Sichuan province was *The Mute and the Cripple*, based on an ancient folk legend about an old man carrying his crippled wife on his back. Later, Dai changed this to a charming dance of an old man carrying his young granddaughter on his back for a promenade through the park. She re-named the dance *Lao Bei Xiao* (The Grandfather Piggy-Backs his Granddaughter). Although this dance appears to be a duet, it was in fact performed by Dai on her own, with a very realistic dummy of the grandfather strapped to her. The grandfather's torso is strapped to the girl's waist, with her own legs appearing to be his. His legs (which seem actually to be hers) are strapped behind her, making it look as if she is really sitting on his shoulders,

Drawing by Ye Chien Yu of Dai in the Jia Rong dance taught by Peng Song

Drawing by Ye Chien Yu of Dai's popluar dance 'Lao Bei Xiao' (Grandfather piggybacks his granddaughter)

playfully fanning herself and plucking a flower from a tree to put in her hair as the old man piggy-backs her through the park. Happily, Dai's enchanting performance of this delightful dance, which remained a favourite with audiences all over China, has been preserved on precious archive film footage of her work.

Items such as this were to form the nucleus of the Chinese dance theatre of the future. Between 1941 and 1946, Dai Ailian gave many performances in Guilin, Guizhou, Chengdu and Chongqing. Then, with the Japanese finally driven out of China and the war in Europe at an end, it was time for Dai to move to Shanghai, and later to Peiping (as Beijing was called at that time) to continue spreading her pioneer work.

In August of 1946, Dai Ailian gave four solo performances in Shanghai. The programme included the Prelude and the Waltz from Fokine's neo-Romantic ballet, *Les Sylphides,* (which Lydia Sokolova had taught Dai in the 1930s, in Margaret Craske's London studio) as well as several dances Dai had choreographed herself, based on Chinese folk dance material. This fusion of Chinese dance with elements of ballet and of modern dance captured the imagination of Shanghai audiences just as it had done in Chongqing. Dai's success in Shanghai resulted in her being invited to the USA as part of a cultural exchange programme. She gave a number of recitals of Chinese dance and, together with her husband Ye Chien Yu – whose drawings and paintings were exhibited in New York – spent a year in America as the guest of the State Department.

Dai returned to Shanghai in the autumn of 1947 to find that a group of her former students from Chongqing had moved to Shanghai where they were eagerly awaiting her return from America. A new recruit had joined the group, a young girl called Wang Ke Fen. Today, Professor Wang is a distinguished dance anthropologist but, in her youth, she had been a member of one of the *Yen Ju Dui* groups – small bands of young singers, actors and musicians, formed in secret by progressive, activist students and politically co-ordinated by Zhou Enlai. They would move audaciously close to the Japanese army's front line, performing patriotic songs and sketches for the price of a meal. Their sole purpose was to boost the morale of the Chinese soldiers and undermine that of the Japanese invaders.

When Dai had left for the USA, some of her Chongqing students had joined Wang Ke Fen's *Yen Ju Dui* performing group in Wuhan. When they moved on to Shanghai to await Dai's return, they persuaded Wang Ke Fen to join them there. I met Professor Wang in the Spring of 2005, in Beijing.

'Ruth the Gleaner', a modern dance choreographed by Dai Ailian. Drawing by Ye Chien Yu

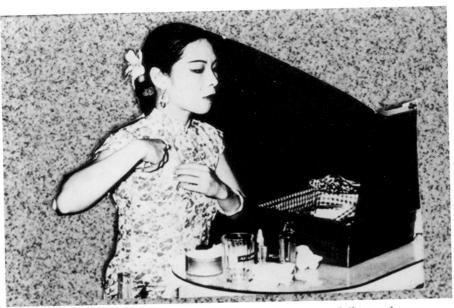

Dai Ailian, backstage in New York after her 1947 performances of Chinese dances

In a long and often emotional interview, she spoke most movingly about working with Dai Ailian.

'We students were all very poor, but determined to work with Dai Ailian. The only venue we could afford was a large room above a Shanghai funeral parlour which the undertaker allowed us to use for our dance classes. Dai taught her own former students from Chongqing, including Wu Yi (who was to come to Dai's assistance later, during the upheavals of the Cultural Revolution) and Dai's first two male students, Peng and Long. Dai had them take on the task of teaching the younger students. So, as well as training dancers, Dai was also giving practical teaching experience to the next generation.'

'None of us had much money, and not only did Dai teach us free of charge, she fed and clothed and even found homes for some of us. One day, I had managed to get my sister in Sichuan to send me a little money. It would not have been enough to buy much more than a few bowls of noodles, but I wanted to give it to Dai. She refused, saying that she hadn't ever paid me for helping her little step daughter with her Chinese homework, so why should I have to pay to learn to dance?'

When word spread of Dai's return to Shanghai, the local Cultural Circle invited her to have her students take part in a performance which was to include a famous pianist and a distinguished opera singer, as well

Dai in Peng Song's choreography inspired by a traditional dance of the Jia Rong people

Yao Ceremonial Dance, Guansi Province. Drawing by Ye Chien Yu

'Alarm' – dance by Dai about a young guerrilla out on patrol. Drawing by Ye Chien Yu

as Kumbarhan and her renowned group of Uyghur folk dancers from Xinjiang. Because of the latter, Dai decided that rather than have her own students also performing folk dances, she would instead revive her dramatic modern dance, *Air Raid*.

'It was always hard for me,' said Wang Ke Fen, 'when Dai revived one of these dances from her Chongqing days. Her older students already knew the choreography, but I had to learn the steps in a hurry. Dai often became impatient with me, making me very nervous at rehearsals. Late at night, I would get the older students out of bed to help me practise the steps so that I could please Dai the next day.' With some passion, Professor Wang now proceeded to describe a typical example of Dai Ailian's integrity and fair-mindedness.

'I was one of four girls asked to learn the part of the mother in the revival of *Air Raid*. One of those four dancers was not only much more experienced than me, she was also Dai's niece. So I was sure it was she who would get to perform the role. In China, it would have seemed natural for a close relative to be favoured in this way. But, to the distress of her niece, Dai chose me – possibly because of my background in drama? But I was less experienced in dancing so, when it came to the part in the dance when the mother runs towards what she thinks is a vision of her dead daughter, I annoyed Dai by asking how many steps I should take?' 'Just run,' she yelled, 'and convince us that you can see your lost child!' 'Well, I must have convinced her, because I got the role.'

Xinjiang, the distant province where Kumbarhan and her Uyghur folk dance group came from, was in the midst of political turmoil. As is still the case today, the Uyghur Moslems, who are of Turkic origin, were trying to gain independence from China. Hoping to quell their uprising, Chiang Kaishek had put one of his fiercest Kuomintang generals in charge of Xinjiang province, unaware that this shady character was actually a secret Communist. It was he who had arranged for Kumbarhan and her dancers to perform in Shanghai. But as well as being politically devious, he was not averse to a little financial malpractice. As Professor Wang put it: 'That corrupt Kuomintang general played a dirty trick on those poor Uyghur folk dancers. He pocketed their share of the box office takings, leaving them stranded in Shanghai. Later, I discovered that it was Mei Lang Feng, the famous Peking Opera artist, who paid their fare back to Xinjiang.'

The rapidly intensifying Civil War left Chiang Kaishek little time to re-establish full control over far-flung areas such as Xinjiang, or to deal with those of his men secretly loyal to Mao Zedong's Communists. The political waters were constantly being muddied by the double game both sides were playing. Such was the atmosphere in which Dai and her dancers had to work. Yet they and many other artists in Shanghai somehow managed to keep going.

In 1948 Dai and her husband were to move to Beijing. Before leaving, Dai ensured that her most promising Shanghai students would be able to continue their dance training with Sukolsky, the émigré White Russian teacher. But she had first to persuade him to agree to teach her students for much less money than the American dollar fees some Russian teachers were able to extract from among the more affluent of the little band of Shanghai ballet hopefuls.

In Beijing, Dai Ailian taught Modern Dance (based on the Sigurd Leeder technique she had studied at Dartington in the late thirties) as well as Chinese folk dance to the students in the Sports department of the Peiping Teachers College and to the music students in the Arts and Music Department of the Peiping Art Academy.

In January of 1949 the People's Liberation Army finally entered Beijing. As news spread of their imminent approach Dai, who was recovering from flu at the time, leapt out of bed, jumped onto her bicycle and headed for Beijing's West Gate to join in the welcome for the liberators. Before proceeding further into the city, the weary soldiers rested for a while in Beihai park. Excited groups of students spotted Dai (whom they knew from their folk dance classes) and rushed up to her shouting 'Please come and dance in the park to comfort and entertain our army.' 'Naturally I was only too happy to do this,' Dai told me, saying that '...many years later, on a visit to the Shengli oil fields in Shangdong province, the local Party Secretary recalled seeing me dance that day in Beihai park and told me how much it had meant to him and his fellow soldiers'.

At the same time as Dai was welcoming the troops at Beijing's West Gate, her former student, Peng Song (who had been travelling in one of the outlying areas already captured by the PLA) was triumphantly beating a drum as he marched ahead of a column of soldiers advancing from the opposite side of the city. Teacher and student were re-united in Tiananmen Square where, just a few months later, Mao Zedong was to proclaim the founding of the People's Republic of China to a crowd of some half a million jubilant citizens.

In the spring of that year, Dai Ailian was chosen as one of the delegates to the Paris-Prague Peace Conference. Dai has particularly fond memories of the warm welcome given to the Chinese delegation by the residents of Prague. 'The Czechs had been enthusiastically monitoring every stage of the Red Army's progress through China. Many Prague homes even kept a map of China on the wall, planting a tiny red flag to mark the location of each Chinese town and city as it was liberated by the Red Army.'

One of the Peace Conference meetings was suddenly interrupted to announce the liberation of Nanjing. The scenes of euphoria which greeted this announcement must have been fuelled in part by the Chinese delegates' bitter memories of the horrific massacre perpetrated in that particular city by the Japanese, in 1937, the now notorious Rape of Nanjing. The slaughter of hundreds of thousands of Chinese in Nanjing over a period of six weeks had been one of the most reprehensible acts of the Sino-Japanese war. Women were raped, children bayonetted, men forced to dig the trenches into which they were to be machine-gunned. The Japanese even conducted chemical experiments on some of their Chinese prisoners although, to this day, many still deny that this ever happened.

As soon as possible, Dai and her fellow Peace Conference delegates set off for Beijing. More good news, including that of the expulsion of the Kuomintang from Shanghai, was to reach them during the long train journey home. Describing some of the excitement she experienced when she got back to Beijing, Dai said: 'Everyone seemed to want to dance. I found myself perched on a table in the open air, directing a folk dance session with two hundred students. The oldest was about forty, the youngest just fourteen years of age. Soon after this, I took part in the collective choreography for a huge celebratory pageant, *The Victory of the Chinese People.'*

The early 1950s saw a growing nation-wide interest in and enthusiasm for Chinese folk song and dance of every type, from that of the ethnic Han (who form the majority of the population of China) to that of remote minorities, such as the Uyghurs, the Mongolians, the Tibetans and the Yao people. With China finally freed both from Japanese aggression and earlier Western economic exploitation, there was now a major revival of interest in the nation's cultural heritage. This was enthusiastically supported by the new Ministry of Culture which, between 1953 and 1957, organised and financed numerous arts festivals throughout the country. Dai Ailian was to play a central role in all of this, both as a performer and as a choreographer.

As early as 1950 Ouyang Yuqian, a male performer of female roles in the ancient traditional art of Kunqu opera, had composed the music for

'Doves of Peace', Beijing, 1950. One of the earliest Chinese ballets. The soloist was Dai Ailian

Dai giving a dance class to factory workers

the first Chinese ballet, *Doves of Peace*. This was largely choreographed by Dai Ailian who also performed the symbolic central role of a dove which had been shot down but was then found and lovingly nursed back to health by a worker. The other performers were students from the Central Drama Academy, with limited dance experience, mainly in folk dance; but the choreography for the Dove was more balletic, with Dai dancing on pointe.

In 1952 the Central Folk Song and Dance ensemble was founded, with Dai as director. For this group she choreographed some of the most admired dance works of the time. They have earned her the reputation of being widely regarded as an icon of Chinese folk dance, the author of its subtle development into a new form of Chinese Dance Theatre, grafting elements of Western theatre dance onto often ancient Chinese folk material. What is remarkable is that Dai Ailian did this without losing the essence or the integrity of the original folk forms. Nowhere was this more clearly exemplified than in her mesmeric 1953 version of the *Lotus Dance*.

Inspired by a simple peasant dance from Shangxi, Dai turned this into an ensemble for a group of young women. She enriched the dancers' upper body movement with the use of épaulement, the three-dimensional effect created in ballet by the subtle counter-movement of the shoulders. The effect of the lotus flowers floating on water was cleverly made by the 'invisible' footwork of the dancers. With their feet hidden under floor-length skirts, the dancers appear to be progressing as if by magic, the silky smoothness of their movement belying the myriad miniscule steps they are having to make as they weave in and out of intricate choreographic formations, to the accompaniment of a song proclaiming the qualities of peace and tranquility.

In 1955 Dai created the strangely exotic duet, *Flying Apsaras*. Apsaras are the 'celestial beings' depicted on the frescoes found in the famous Dunhuang caves in Gansu province. Basing the dance initially on the images found in these ancient caves, dating from the time of the Tang dynasty, Dai further developed the movement for her choreography from two other sources: one was a scarf dance she had seen being performed by a girl from one of the Minority groups in North East China; the other was a dance performed by the Beijing Opera singer, Mei Langfeng. Combining elements from both of these sources with the Dunhuang cave images of 'celestial beings', Dai's dancers used extremely long scarves, functioning as 'wings', but in a less obvious, stylised manner. These scarves were manipulated by the dancers with breathtaking skill as they gyrated to the eerie sounds of Lu Xin's specially composed musical score. Originally conceived as a solo, Dai then turned this dance into a more complex duet form, drawing this time on aspects of Laban's space-movement theories.

As an expatriate Chinese child, born in Trinidad, Dai had originally had very little knowledge or understanding of Chinese culture or history. As a dance student in London in the 1930s, she had remarked that she was able to see performances of Spanish dance, Indian dance and dances of various other nationalities, but never any Chinese dance. So, from those early student days, it had been her ambition, some day, to go to China and research authentic Chinese folk dance. As we have now seen, this she did with rare determination and success, travelling to some of the remotest areas of China's 'Borderlands', inhabited by the numerous Minority peoples. She also studied the dances of the Han majority, helping to develop nation-wide interest in the many different styles of the Yangge, or 'planting the rice' dance. It is important to stress that, in addition to her work in adapting folk dance forms for the stage, Dai was also instrumental in encouraging ordinary people to participate in simple, recreational folk dance gatherings

Having achieved her ambition to 're-discover' and popularise authentic Chinese dance, Dai and China were now both ready to tackle classical ballet on a serious professional scale.

CHAPTER SIX

ESTABLISHING CLASSICAL BALLET IN CHINA

Following the Russian revolution of 1917, large numbers of refugees fleeing the Bolsheviks arrived in China. Initially, the majority made for Harbin but, gradually, many moved on to other cities, notably Shanghai, Tianjin, and even British ruled Hong Kong. Among these refugees there were several Russian ballet dancers and teachers, including Georgi Goncharov and Vera Volkova. Both later made their way to Western Europe where Goncharov taught at the Sadler's Wells Ballet School in London, whilst Volkova not only taught the Sadler's Wells Ballet Company but also played an important role in the subsequent development of the Danish Royal Ballet Company, in Copenhagen. But in the 1920s Volkova and Goncharov were still refugees, scraping a living in Shanghai, teaching ballet privately and staging the occasional dance performance.

Among their pupils was the young Margot Fonteyn (or Peggy Hookham as she was still called) whose father was at that time stationed in China. Fonteyn, of course, was later destined to become the prima ballerina assoluta of London's Royal Ballet Company. There were several other, less distinguished, émigré Russian ballet teachers working in China during the 1930s and the 1940s, including George Toropov, Edouard Elirov and the Sukolskis, husband and wife. It was in the Sukolskis' Shanghai studio that Dai Ailian, in exchange for teaching them some Chinese folk dances, was later able to keep up her own classical ballet technique.

Although she had done some ballet teaching herself in Chongqing, and later in Shanghai, the focus of Dai's work in her early days in China had been on researching and developing folk material. She had also continued to include the occasional classical ballet item in her solo dance recitals. However, in those days, apart from a few expatriate Europeans living in China, it would have been only the occasional, sophisticated urban Chinese who would have shown any interest at all in ballet – an art form then still totally unknown to the vast majority of the Chinese population. It is therefore all the more remarkable that, in 1954, the Chinese government set in train the establishment of a professional Dance School with a Teacher Training programme.

During the mid and late 1940s, as the Chinese were tenaciously fighting their way towards liberation from the Japanese invaders and the resolution of their own Civil War, the people's nationalistic fervour was increasingly being expressed in the form of song and dance and in little patriotic dramatic sketches. Many *danwei* (or Chinese Work Units, such as factories, agricultural co-operatives and industrial complexes) had their own dance groups, as did most army units. As one elderly gentleman who, as a young army recruit, had enjoyed performing in his platoon's dance group, put it to me: 'China seemed to be going dance crazy.' It was from these amateur performance groups, as well as from schools and universities throughout China that the first students for the future Central Ballet School were recruited.

A selection from among the most talented of these students were given a rigorous dance training with the idea, after graduation, of building up a professional ballet company. In 1954, Dai Ailian (who between 1949 and 1953 had held the posts of Head of Dance in the Arts Department of North China University and of the Central Song and Folk Dance Ensemble) was appointed to the important new post of Principal of the new Beijing Dance School (today a department of the Beijing Dance Academy).

Dai Ailian held the post of Principal of the Beijing Dance School for over a decade. It is interesting to note the comments made about that school, and about Dai Ailian, by Marie Rambert, the Director of London's Ballet Rambert Company, which had performed in Beijing in 1957. In her autobiography, *Quicksilver*, (Macmillan, London, 1972) Rambert writes that: 'I was most impressed by that wonderful school, with its perfect curriculum, and I felt proud of my pupil'. Rambert had indeed been one of Dai Ailian's teachers in London, in the 1930s; but she had not taken 'Eileen' – as Rambert used to call her – into the Ballet Rambert Company, feeling that '... people would notice her for unimportant things like the difference in colour and features' (an interesting insight into the racial attitudes still prevailing in 1930s England!). 'I advised her to go back to China and teach, which she was excellent at, and perhaps found a company of her own.'

As well as classical ballet and Chinese folk dance, the Beijing Dance School also taught classes in so-called Chinese Classical Dance. This is actually a hybrid form based on ancient traditions, stemming in part from some of the acrobatic and mimetic elements found in traditional Chinese Opera. Commenting on that aspect of the Beijing Dance School's curriculum, Marie Rambert wrote that '... they have evolved a complete system of training, based on the deepest features of Chinese tradition, and so it can be preserved, just as our European tradition is.'

The founding of the Beijing Dance School had coincided with a period of very close co-operation between the Soviet Union and the People's Republic of China. Thousands of Chinese were sent to study in the Soviet Union and large numbers of Soviet Russian industrial and agricultural experts were despatched to China to help with the rapid development of the country along the lines of the Soviet model.

Renowned as the Russians are for their pre-eminence in the field of classical ballet, it was only natural that the Soviet experts sent to China included several Soviet ballet teachers. Among the most influential were Viktor Tsaplin (from the Bolshoi Ballet in Moscow) and Pyotr Gusev (from the Kirov Ballet in Leningrad) as well as the character dance teacher Tamara Leisovich and the pas de deux teacher Nicolai Sebrenikov, also from Leningrad. These fine teachers – and especially Gusev – eventually accomplished remarkable things with the fledgling Central Ballet Company (which grew out of the Beijing Dance School) and of which Dai Ailian was the Artistic Director from 1963 to 1966.

However, by all accounts, it seems that the first Moscow instructor sent to teach the Chinese the carefully structured Soviet Russian training system was not universally admired. For one thing (and no doubt on orders from Moscow) she set out the framework for a five or six year training course, as opposed to the eight or nine-year course of training used in Russia itself. In retrospect, the accelerated training programme used by their first Soviet teacher has been blamed by some people for the high rate of injury among some of the earliest Chinese ballet students.

Be that as it may, it is important to understand that the Soviet Russian method of ballet training which, at its best, is universally acknowledged to produce some superb results, is more rigidly systematised than was the dance training Dai Ailian had encountered as a ballet student in London. Therefore, so as to familiarise herself with the Soviet system, Dai participated in the initial (accelerated) teacher-training course conducted by that first Soviet tutor.However, it was not until the arrival of Gusev, with his much more refined and artistically sensitive approach that Dai felt able to appreciate fully the merits of the Soviet Russian training system. This was based on the work of the distinguished Russian teacher, Agrippina Vaganova.

Vaganova had herself been a private pupil of the great Italian teacher, Enrico Cecchetti, and Dai would undoubtedly have recognized in the Vaganova work, as taught by Gusev, aspects of the Cecchetti Method

Dai teaching a Cecchetti class to the Central Ballet of China, Beijing 1965

which she had studied in London with Cecchetti's disciple, Margaret Craske. So it is mainly through Gusev that Dai was able to absorb the best qualities of the Soviet Russian schooling which, to this day, still forms the basis of ballet training in China.

As an enthusiastic pre-teen ballet pupil in Trinidad, Dai Ailian had displayed something of a natural, if precocious, flair for teaching. Yet once she began professional dance training in London, and later at Dartington, her focus was entirely on becoming a dancer. In fact, she recalls one of the Cecchetti Society's London teachers, Mabel Ryan, trying in vain to persuade her to join a pedagogy course. 'I want to be a dancer, not a teacher,' was her reaction. Now, in China, she made every effort to assimilate the teaching principles espoused by the Soviet ballet experts although, in her own teaching, she remained loyal to the Cecchetti principles she had learnt in London, from Craske and Rambert.

Indeed, it was with the intention of having some of Cecchetti's work re-introduced at the Beijing Dance School that Dai Ailian invited me to teach the students at that school and to conduct seminars for their teachers. This was in the Winter of 2000 to 2001, and again in the spring of 2005. The older teachers on the staff of the school seemed to be genuinely interested in re-discovering aspects of the type of training they had experienced in the 1950s, under Dai Ailian, while the younger teachers and the students found the challenge of Cecchetti's faster footwork as well as that of his subtly co-ordinated *port de bras* (exercises for the carriage of the arms) genuinely stimulating.

Nevertheless, from the mid-1950s, the training of the students at the Beijing Dance School and later that of the dancers in the Central Ballet Company was to be supervised by Soviet Russian teachers. One of the reasons for the original, accelerated programme according to which the early students at the Beijing Dance School were trained was no doubt due to the fact that both the Chinese and the Russian governments were equally anxious to see some rapid results from their new, joint balletic venture. 'How long will it take you to be ready to stage a performance of *Swan Lake*?', the Chinese premier, Zhou Enlai, had enquired. He was told it would take at least five years. 'In fact, we did it in just over four,' recalls Dai Ailian. 'Gusev was a slave driver,' she adds 'but he was also very clever and practical in the way he adapted his staging of the most famous of Russian ballets to suit our particular circumstances and abilities.'

At the time of the initial performance of the Chinese *Swan Lake*, the male dancers in the fledgling company were still very inexperienced in the art of partnering. The Prince in this ballet, as well as being a skillful partner (strong enough to be able to perform some strenuous 'lifts' in the pas de deux with the Swan Queen) has also to perform a technically demanding solo. Gusev chose Liu Qingtang for the role of the Prince, in spite of the fact that this young man had hardly had any serious ballet training; on the other hand, he was the only one strong enough to 'lift' the ballerina. So Gusev compromised by cutting the male solo in order to be assured of a capable partner for Bai Shuxiang, China's first Swan Queen.

I was told this story, with some amusement, on the night in December 2000 when I attended a rather curious Gala Performance given on the enormous stage of Beijing's Great Hall of the People, during which the pas de deux from Act Two of *Swan Lake* was performed *simultaneously* by no fewer than five couples! A telling example not only of the Chinese dancers' rapid progress (largely due to the pas de deux coaching of Nicolai Sebrenikov) but also of the Chinese taste for larger than life spectacle. Nowadays, of course, most male graduates of the Beijing Dance School are able both to master the technique of the Prince's *Swan Lake* solo and also to tackle the 'lifts' in any classical pas de deux.

It would be impossible to over-state the contribution made by Soviet Russian teachers and ballet masters to the development of classical ballet in China. The excellent standard of ballet technique, both in the Beijing Dance School and in the National Ballet Company, undoubtedly has its roots in the teaching methods the Chinese adapted from the Soviet Russian model. It is the Chinese dancers' excellent technique which underpins the high standard of performance in the National Ballet Company's presentations of the nineteenth century classics. In addition to *Swan Lake*, the Russians also staged *Giselle, Le Corsaire* and *La fille mal gardée* for the Company. Much less valuable was the Soviet Russian contribution to and influence on the development of new choreography in China.

As well as staging the classics, Gusev also conducted classes in choreography but, as was also the case in Soviet Russia, these were more lessons in the craft of the arrangement and the dramatic staging of dance than in the creative art of choreography as it is understood in the West. The prevailing fashion in Eastern Bloc countries with Communist regimes favoured the staging of three-act ballets, usually structured according to a standard formula. In Act One the characters were introduced; Act Two consisted mainly in some sort of conflict or contradiction between these characters; this was then resolved in Act Three. In tune with the revolutionary ideals of the People's Republic, all new choreography in China had to be created collectively, with several dancers and musicians contributing to the choreography and to the musical composition of the new work, supervised and guided by Gusev.

An early example of this type of collectively created ballet was *The Maid of the Sea*. The story of this ballet concerned the adventures of a hunter in his quest to rescue a sea nymph from a mountain demon and it provided many opportunities for the inclusion of folk dance and acrobatics. The Soviet Russian 'recipe' used in the creation of this work was undoubtedly at odds with Dai Ailian's concept of choreography, nurtured as it had been in the climate of individual creative freedom of the 1930s English ballet world. Nevertheless, for the next decade, 'collective creativity' was to be the officially sanctioned mode for making new work in China.

During the late 1950s, Mao Zedong was becoming increasingly critical of what he saw as Moscow's 'revisionist' idea of socialism. He had always seen the creation of a new Chinese national culture as an essential part of a China which would at last be totally free from the political oppression and the economic exploitation of the West. More than a decade earlier, in his 1942 'Talks' at the Yenan Forum on Literature and Art, Mao had proclaimed that 'Proletarian Literature and Art are part of the whole revolutionary cause; they are, as Lenin said, cogs and wheels in the revolutionary machine.'

Mao's idealised vision of a truly egalitarian, socialist society was again to dictate policy from about 1960 when, because of conflicting ideological positions, the increasingly fragile relationship between Moscow and Beijing finally broke down completely. Russia recalled all the Soviet experts working in China, including Gusev and the rest of the Russian ballet staff. Their sudden departure could have had disastrous consequences for the fledgling Chinese Ballet. Luckily, during this difficult period of transition, the training in the School and the future development of the Company were assured under the sensitive guidance of Dai Ailian.

Shi Shenfang, who had been trained by the Russians, was now able to take on some of the teaching, while three of the graduates who had earlier been sent to Russia to further their studies, now returned to Beijing to play their part in the Company's development. They were Jiang Zuhui, Wang Xixian and Ma Yunhong. They brought back from Russia two full-length ballets, *The Fountain of Tears* and *Notre Dame de Paris*, both of which became popular additions to the Company's 1963 repertoire. More importantly, the Russians had also given them some instruction in the art of choreography and Jiang Zuhui in particular was later to reveal a real talent for this in one of her finest works, *The New Year Sacrifice*. This is the tale of a tragic widow, forced into marriage with a young farmer who finally wins her love through kindness. The celebrations preceding the arrival of the bride provided the opportunity for some delightful folk dancing, dramatically interrupted by the unveiling of the bride, bound and gagged, with a cloth in her mouth. This ballet was much admired by both the New York and the London dance critics during the Central Ballet Company's 1986 foreign tour.

The guest appearances by the English ballerina, Beryl Grey, in February and March of 1964, were among the most notable events to take place during the period following the departure of the Russians. In her book, *Through the Bamboo Curtain* (Collins, London, 1965), Miss Grey has given a detailed description of ballet in Beijing, as well as a charming and insightful account of life in China in the mid-1960s. In addition to inviting Beryl Grey to appear in *Swan Lake* (the first appearance of an English dancer with the Chinese company), Dai Ailian had also asked her to stage the whole of *Les Sylphides*. (Previously the dancers had only performed a few solo extracts from that ballet). Beryl Grey's visit was remarkably successful and she has written eloquently and in some detail both about the high standard of the dancers and the enthusiastic response of the audiences. Yet, at the same time as Beijing was responding so favourably to Beryl Grey's visit, it was announced that ballet, together with all the other arts in China, was now to concentrate on works dealing with 'socially relevant' contemporary themes.

Ballet in China was to be officially 'reformed' according to the new political climate and various 'propaganda ballets' were staged, the most important of which, *The Red Detachment of Women* was to remain popular for half a century.

Originally made as a film and later converted into a three act ballet, *The Red Detachment of Women* was based on a true story. The action took place on Hainan Island, in southern China, during the second Chinese Civil War of 1927 to 1937. It tells the story of a young slave girl, Wu Ching Hua, who escapes from her cruel master, Nan Ba Tien, and seeks refuge among the Communist army in the 'liberated area'. She joins a unit of the Red Army called the Red Detachment of Women, becomes a courageous and tenacious fighter and, eventually, after the Hero, the Communist Party Representative Hong Chung Chin is killed, she takes his place as Leader. The ballet, originally called *The Red Women's Army* and then renamed *The Red Detachment of Women* was premiered in Beijing on 1st October 1964, the fifteenth anniversary of the proclamation of the People's Republic.

In preparation for this iconic, landmark production, and in accordance with Mao Zedong's dictum 'Learn from the People', the dancers from Beijing's Central Ballet Company were despatched to Hainan Island to learn at first hand of the Red Army Women's heroic deeds, before being sent into the field to be taught by the army how to handle guns realistically.

The other important revolutionary ballet, *The White Haired Girl*, was also staged in 1964, this time at the Shanghai Dance School. Based on various folk tales and on an opera of the same name, this ballet tells the story of a peasant girl forced into slavery by a wealthy landlord. He rapes and torments her until, in despair, her jet black hair turned white from grief, she manages to escape and to hide in a cave until the evil landlord is killed by the soldiers of the victorious Red Army. Liberated by them, she joins the revolutionary struggle. *The Red Detachment of Women* and *The White Haired Girl* were the two major ballets reflecting the ideological fervour dominating China during the mid-1960s. In these 'revolutionary' ballets, pointe work was used in a radically different way from that of traditional classical/romantic ballet. In the new Chinese context, pointe work

Dancers of the Central Ballet of China being trained by the army in preparation for the ballet 'The Red Detachment of Women'

The Central Ballet of China (now the National Ballet) in 'The Red Detachment of Women'

expressed the notions of power, strength and a sense of triumph. The men's dances paralleled these emotions with their virtuoso spins and leaps.

Like all new ballets in China during the sixties and the early seventies, *The Red Detachment of Women* was a communal creation, with choreography by Li Chen Xiang, Jiang Zu Hui and Wang Xi Xian, and with music composed by Wang Zu Qiang and Du Ming Xin. With its ranks of gun-toting female soldiers in pointe shoes, its huge groups of fierce guerillas and militia men, and its high-minded heroics, this was indeed the epitome of the 'ideologically correct propaganda ballet'.

During one of the early rehearsals for *The Red Detachment of Women* Dai Ailian (then still the Artistic Director of the Central Ballet Company) was informed that an important woman was coming to visit the Company. Little did Dai realise what ominous consequences that visit was to have, both for the future of the arts in China in general and for her own, personal existence in particular. The important visitor (although Dai did not realise this at the time) was Mao Zedong's third wife, Jiang Qing who, as one of the notorious Gang of Four, was soon to play such a prominent part in China's impending Cultural Revolution.

However, before embarking on the often harrowing tale of the Chinese Cultural Revolution, with its disastrous effects on all aspects of Chinese society, there is one other area of Dai Ailian's work which was and still is of importance both in relation to ballet and to folk dance: Labanotation in China.

CHAPTER SEVEN

LABANOTATION IN CHINA

Movement notation, one of the subjects Dai Ailian had been studying at Dartington just before the outbreak of the Second World War, represents just one area of Rudolf von Laban's study of all aspects of movement. This ranged from analysing the efficiency of work patterns in industry to recording the most complex and intricate of dance sequences. Laban's system of movement notation, originally called Kinetographie and subsequently developed into what is now known as Labanotation, is used all over the world to record many different types of choreography; it also proved to be an invaluable tool for Dai Ailian in her task of recording for posterity the folk dances of the people living in some of China's most remote borderland areas. Several of these dances have now been published in Labanotation.

With her usual enthusiasm for everything and everyone connected with dance, Dai was also instrumental in promoting the study of Labanotation throughout China, and in fostering its use in a wide variety of areas, from dance to ethnographic research.

Initially, Dai taught basic, Elementary Labanotation to a few of her students. One of these was Wu Jingshu, or Lollie as she is popularily known. Being an expert linguist, it was Lollie who took on the task of translating Laban's technical terminology into Chinese. During one of Dai's absences abroad, it was Lollie who continued Dai's work of introducing basic concepts of Labanotation to increasingly large numbers of enthusiasts. Later, Dai began teaching the more complex Intermediate level of Labanotation to the most able and committed of her students. In 1983, this was to lead to the official founding of the Labanotation Society of China, under the auspices of the Chinese Dancers' Association. Thanks to the work of this organisation, the interest in and the influence of Labanotation continued to be championed throughout China. In the late 1980s, Eileen Fox, of the Dance Notation Bureau in New York, and Carl Wolz, another internationally recognised authority on the subject, started teaching the Advanced level of Labanotation to a select group of some thirty students from various parts of the country.

One of the particularly complex areas of Labanotation involves recording the handling of properties, such as the intricate use of fans

Yi nationality Baozipo villagers performing their 'Moon Dance', in 1987

found in some folk dances. For generations, folk dancers have manipulated such properties since childhood and do so quite naturally and with apparent ease. Yet, recording this type of movement accurately in notation can be quite tricky. On one famous occasion, when recording a particular Chinese folk dance involving the simultaneous manipulation of a fan with one hand whilst twirling a handkerchief with the other one (all in precise time with the music, and in strict co-ordination with the dancer's footwork), it took a particular student three hours to complete the task of notating in detail the tracing of the track of the fan and the handkerchief along circular paths through different planes of movement. The fact that Carl Wolz was then able to decipher these notated movements accurately, and to perform them (albeit in slow motion) in just a few minutes was a clear vindication of the efficacy of this system and of its value in helping to preserve aspects of China's cultural heritage.

The enormous geographical and climatic diversity of this vast country has, of course, influenced the characteristics of individual Chinese folk dances. Farmer or city dweller, peasant or factory worker, the way people dance is inevitably influenced by where they live and by the type of work they do. Living in the steep, mountainous regions of Tibet, or along the sea coast of Guangdong; scraping a living somewhere in the remote

MOON DANCE

The Sani sect of the YI nationality said they learnt this dance from
the Assi sect. Hence the similarity. The boys all strum on string
instruments, big and small, and the bamboo flute plays the melody. It
is done in two lines, or in two circles, the boys facing the girls who are
in the outer circle. The youth of the Sani people of Baozipo village,
Baodaoshao-Baozipo Area, Qiubei County, Wenshan Prefecture,
Yunnan Province do their courting when there is moonlight, dancing
by the mountain-side.

(Introduction: 2 Bars 3/4, 2/4)

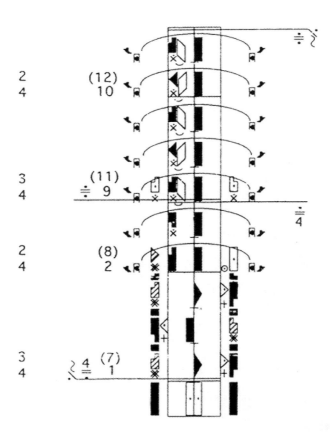

Dai's Labanotation recording of the Baozipo villagers 'Moon Dance'

SHOUNAN QINBU
(Good Fortune)

"There are 130,000 Lamas in the temple east of the Eastern Sea continuing Zong Gerba's vocation."

(Introduction: 2 bars)

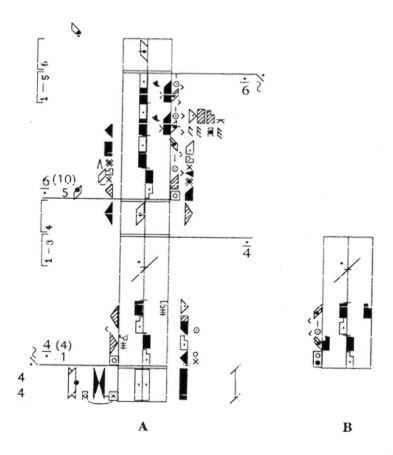

A   B

Dai's Labanotation recording of the Tibetan folk dance 'Shounan Qinbu' (Good Fortune)

3. SHOUNAN QINBU
(Good Fortune)

Musical notation for the Tibetan folk dance "Shounan Qinbu' (Good Fortune)

plains of Xinjiang or enjoying nature's abundance among the fertile fields of Sichuan can affect the way people dance. In studying these differences, Chinese academics in the field of ethnographic research have identified and analysed some two hundred and seventy separate folk dance movements; from these they have compiled fifty basic combinations. One of Madame Dai's students undertook the task of recording all this material for publication in the first book on Chinese folk dance to include the use of Labanotation, giving full detail of the dynamics and musical timing involved (in addition to the more usual basic written description of the movements, supplemented with some drawings or photographs). At the other end of the scale are those teachers who use some of the basic Labanotation concepts, in a simplified form, as a tool for teaching children how to explore space, using varied movement levels in their creative dance sessions.

The Modern Dance Department of the Beijing Dance Academy and those of many other Chinese colleges and universities now use Labanotation as part of their teacher-training programmes. This equips their students to read and understand the various types of movement material that have been recorded in Labanotation. As one of China's Laban enthusiasts put it to me: 'The use of Labanotation helps to broaden the mind. It involves more than just deciphering the notation and helps us to appreciate all the intricacies of each particular movement style. This

Dai Ailian (fourth from left) on one of her field trips to collect folk dance material from China's Ethnic Minority Peoples

was especially evident to us when, as dancers basically schooled in the Soviet Russian tradition of classical ballet, we were first introduced to the very different Bournonville style of the Royal Danish Ballet.'

At the time of writing, the vast repertoire of Enrico Cecchetti's work is also in the process of being recorded in Labanotation. That will eventually make this important material accessible to those dancers and teachers in China who, because of the prevalence of the Soviet Russian balletic legacy have in the past had only limited access to what Dai Ailian rightly considers to be a vital component of the classical ballet canon. Writing in the programme of the *Tribute to Ashton and Cecchetti* presented in the Linbury Theatre of the Royal Opera House in London's Covent Garden, on 12th November 2000, Dai Ailian said that: 'Through Margaret Craske's teachings I am forever indebted to Enrico Cecchetti, the great Master whose teaching method – passed down by dancers from generation to generation – is so important to the world of classical ballet. We in China are very proud to be part of that great heritage.'

Thus, the legacies of Dai Ailian's two great heroes, Enrico Cecchetti and Rudolph von Laban, are being united through the medium of Labanotation, as have been her two great passions, Chinese folk dance and classical ballet. But how were Dai Ailian's life's work and her unique contribution to Chinese culture going to be affected by China's impending Cultural Revolution?

Traditional costume of Tibetan dancers (© Dai Ailian)

CHAPTER EIGHT

THE CULTURAL REVOLUTION

The root causes of China's notorious Cultural Revolution can be traced back in part to the failure of Mao Zedong's forced communisation of the countryside, the so-called Great Leap Forward (1958-1960). This was part of his disastrous attempt to hasten the industrialisation of what was basically still a peasant society. The government's subsequent efforts to recover quickly and efficiently from what the Chinese still refer to as those 'three difficult years' began to be seen by Mao as a reactionary return to bourgeois values and corrupt bureaucracy. In short, a betrayal of his pure communist ideals. The Cultural Revolution which Mao then set in train in 1966 (and which was to last for the best part of a decade) aimed to reverse this state of affairs by means of a total transformation of Chinese society.

The ideology underpinning the Cultural Revolution was the perceived need to eliminate the 'Four Olds': 'old customs, old habits, old culture, old thinking'. In fact, as the footsoldiers of the Cultural Revolution, the dreaded Red Guards, took over the whole country, the result was a complete breakdown of rational, civilised behaviour. Intellectuals and artists were among the many people, from all walks of life, who were side-lined, dismissed and persecuted. At best, they were exiled to the countryside to be 're-educated' through manual labour; at worst, many were killed, sometimes beaten to death.

Some of the worst excesses of the Cultural Revolution took place during the initial four-year period; but its immediate ramifications lasted for over a decade and, more than a quarter of a century later, they were still affecting some aspects of Chinese life. A case in point relates to someone whom, out of respect for Dai Ailian's wishes, I will only refer to as Mr X. In an unguarded moment, Dai spoke to me about him, briefly and with barely concealed bitterness. She then quickly dismissed the subject as 'unimportant'. However, a source close to her explained to me that this Mr X was the man who, during the Cultural Revolution, had falsely accused Dai of being a spy. Apparently, according to my source, '... he never apologised properly afterwards'. This man still occupies a senior position in the Chinese dance world and, as he is a member of the Communist Party, it seems that Dai continued to feel that he had the potential to harm her. Considering the very high regard in which Dai is held by the authorities and her own important (albeit later only symbolic) position as adviser to the National Ballet, Dai's continued fears of Mr X were almost certainly unfounded. Yet, for many people of Dai Ailian's generation, the Cultural Revolution continues to cast a long shadow.

Most prominent among the ultra-radical leaders of the Cultural Revolution, the Gang of Four, was Jiang Qing. A former cinema starlet, she became Mao's wife and, as such, wielded enormous power. She used that power ruthlessly in her drive to impose her radical ideological ideas on all aspects of the arts in China.

Jiang Qing (Madame Mao) took control of the Beijing Opera, the Central Philharmonic Orchestra and the Central Ballet Company, ostensibly with the serious ideological purpose of turning these institutions – which she saw as representative of a decadent bourgeois mentality – into radical, socialist, proletarian organisations. In fact, much of what she did was quite simply absurd. One of her most ridiculous acts – and the one which perhaps most clearly exemplifies her ignorance – related to the work of the Central Philharmonic Orchestra. Jiang Qing ordered the conductor to get rid of the trombones which, she declared, made an 'anti-revolutionary sound'. Worried at the thought of losing these important instruments, the conductor managed to persuade her that the sound she so disliked actually emanated from the tubas, not the trombones. So the tubas were discarded, with comparatively less of a loss!

Similarly idiotic orders were issued to the Central Ballet Company by, for example, the banning of two traditional ballet steps which Madame Mao considered to be 'anti-revolutionary': the *pas de basque* and the *entrechat*. The French technical terminology traditionally used in ballet is internationally accepted; but as she tightened her grip on the Chinese ballet world, Madame Mao also sought to replace that terminology. Images from the natural world such as 'the stance of the heron bird' were now ordered to replace French technical terms such as *en attitude* whilst 'sharp leaps to frighten the enemy' was the sort of militaristic image now used to describe those split jumps the French call *grand écart en l'air*. A more fittingly poetic description was adopted in the place of that iconic ballet term, the *arabesque*: this was now to be known as 'spreading your wings in the welcome breeze'.

Somewhat naively Dai Ailian (when she was still nominally in charge of the ballet company) had not, at first, realised that by talking openly with Mao's wife about ballet matters, she was unwittingly storing up future problems for herself. Once, when Jiang Qing had come to watch an early rehearsal of *The Red Detachment of Women*, the conversation turned to a discussion about the traditional inclusion in many classical ballets of stylised Spanish, Polish or Hungarian dances (and even, as in *The Nutcracker*, a pastiche of a Chinese dance). Not realising both how uneducated and how virulently anti all Western culture Jiang Qing was, Dai Ailian talked openly to her about trying to present such national dances in a more authentic form, rather than in the ersatz style in which they were performed in traditional ballets. What Dai had not yet realised, was that the very notion of wanting to respect the culture of other nations was anathema to Madame Mao. Dai's still somewhat limited command of the Chinese language, together with her foreign accent (she spoke Mandarin with a slight Trinidadian lilt!) also aroused Jiang Qing's antipathy. Little did Dai realise how a seemingly innocuous conversation about the purity of various national dance styles would eventually become the source of a series of accusations to be levelled at her later by Jiang Qing.

To understand the context in which such a bizarre state of affairs could exist, it is necessary to appreciate the lengths to which the leaders of the Cultural Revolution were prepared to go in order to 're-educate' the entire population of China. In its initial stages, the Cultural Revolution was concerned primarily with denouncing those Communist government officials whom Mao suspected of revisionist, bourgeois tendencies. These included a number of his closest comrades, branded by Mao as 'Capitalist Traitors'. Soon, the accusations levelled at these government officials began to be aimed at a variety of other Party Members. But Dai Ailian was not a political person and, unusually for someone in a position of considerable authority, she had never joined the Communist Party. Therefore, in its early stages, the Cultural Revolution had had little direct effect on her. Then, later in 1966, Mao, aided and abetted by his wife, launched an all-out attack on the worlds of Education and the Arts. This was to be the final, determined push to rid Chinese society once and for all of every vestige of bourgeois influence.

The roots of all this can be traced back to the late 1950s when, in an effort to purge China of the so-called 'Rightists' who, in Mao's eyes, were endangering the very existence of China as a true Socialist state, he ordered Party officials to denounce as 'Rightists' 5% of the staff of every *danwei* or Work Unit. This was a horribly crude policy which resulted in many thousands of dreadful injustices. Many intellectuals in influential positions tried to resist Mao's 'Red Line', which called for the abandoning of all Western culture. They attempted to impose their own 'Black Line', which advocated the continuing 'value of learning from the foreigners'. But their struggle was in vain.

Mao, commenting on the ballets performed by the Central Ballet Company, had been heard to say 'Why do I only see foreign princes and ghosts on stage?' Perhaps his wife took that remark as her cue? Soon, anyone and anything with a Western connection became a target for the Red Guards and the Gang of Four (Jiang Qing, Zhang Chunqiao, Yao Wenyuan and Wang Hongwen). Jiang Qing took personal control over all artistic and theatrical life in China, and especially in Beijing. For the next few years, the only major ballets the Central Ballet Company were allowed to perform were the ideologically acceptable *The Red Detachment of Women* and later, *The White Haired Girl*. Similarly politically correct criteria were applied to the so-called 'model' presentations of the Beijing Opera, as well as to the repertoire the Central Philharmonic orchestra were allowed to perform.

Dai Ailian was now gradually sidelined. Initially, she remained as Director of the Central Ballet Company, but only in name. Jiang Qing was now the one really in command. Condemning everything that had been created before 1966, she declared herself to be 'The Banner of the Proletarian Arts'. The following is how Dai Ailian has described the subsequent chain of events: 'Although I was forced to step aside, at first I was not arrested. I was still allowed to sit in at communal meetings of the Ballet Company, which were now presided over by Madame Mao. One day I heard a tape recording of her screaming "Why have you not yet touched Dai Ailian?" That was how she first denounced me. One of her associates then asked "Has she got any historical questions?" meaning was there anything bad I had done in the past against the ideals of the Communist Party?'

'From that day on, they tried to isolate me. They made me write out my history from my birth to the present day. I was made to write this out again and again during the next four or five years. And they cross-questioned me about everything I wrote. I was also made to do manual work, cleaning out the ballet studios and the school dormitories. I was ordered to cut my long hair, and they threatened to shave my head if I did not cut my hair short myself.'

'The workers and the army were now in charge. During one of my interrogation sessions a certain Chinese word was used which I did not understand. I had to look it up in a dictionary. It turned out to be something to do with my army rank. I was surprised, as I had never joined the army; but because I had lived for some time in Chongqing, the city in which the opposition military leader, Chiang Kaishek, had had his military base during the Japanese invasion, they suspected me of having been in the Kuomintang army. I told them I had never joined any army, so I could not answer their repeated questions about my military rank!' Then, in 1970, Dai Ailian was told she was going to be sent to work in the countryside and to be prepared for a long stay. 'So I thought that I was now going to be a farmer for the rest of my life.'

'First I was sent to an experimental agricultural unit. I was over fifty years of age, so they thought I was too old to learn. I was told to tidy the orchard, to pick up leaves and twigs. They wouldn't even let me prune the fruit trees. They said I was too stupid to learn how to do it. Madame Mao had also taken control of the Beijing Opera Company, and among the artists she had sent to work on the land was a very famous opera singer whom I knew well. We had been together as members of a Chinese Cultural Delegation sent to India, Burma and Indonesia before the Cultural Revolution. Now I saw this distinguished artist carrying heavy loads and working in the fields in the midday heat. Whenever I greeted him, he would look around nervously to make sure we were not being watched. I heard later that he had been savagely beaten by the Red Guards.'

'Later, together with a Ballet Company unit of about thirty people, I was sent to another farm. There I was made to weed the vegetable garden. It was winter; I caught cold and I was bed-ridden three times in one year. They accused me of pretending to be ill. They forced me to get up and made me climb up and down stairs. I was described as a monster and was sent off to look after the pigs. I liked my pigs. I collected swill from the kitchen to feed them. It had to be heated to a certain temperature and my hand got infected testing it. Some of the other workers took pity on me. One of these was the old Ballet Company chauffeur. He would sometimes secretly slip a cake into my pocket. Another worker, a plumber, laid a pipe to transport the water I had previously had to carry in two buckets attached to a long pole held across my shoulders. We all tried to help one another, but those were hard times, especially in winter.'

Once Madame Mao had reorganised the Ballet Company along what she considered to be suitably proletarian lines, she decided to give Dai Ailian a new task; this was in connection with a planned tour to Albania. This involved preparing the dancers' pointe shoes; for although so many aspects of Western dance had been jettisoned, the patriotic ballerinas in *The Red Detachment of Women* still danced on their toes. So someone was needed to darn their pointe shoes. (So as to be able to dance on the tips of their toes, ballet dancers wear special pointe shoes. These are soft satin slippers which have been stiffened with a papier mâché block and a special type of glue. The block soon becomes soft and begins to wear out. So, traditionally, ballerinas used to darn the tips of their satin pointe shoes with strong silk thread. This helped to lengthen the life of the shoe. Normally, a dancer would have darned a pair of pointe shoes gradually, over a period of a day or two, usually during breaks between rehearsals or when relaxing at home. It can be quite a time-consuming chore.) But Jiang Qing was a hard taskmaster and she managed to find a new way to torment Dai Ailian.

'I was given a large pile of pointe shoes to darn and was forced to stay awake for several days, until the job was done. All I was given to eat was a bowl of beans at midnight. I was then allowed to rest for two days before being given another batch of pointe shoes to darn. I ended up with a frozen shoulder.'

Compared with the savage treatment meted out to many other artists, intellectuals and professionals of every type during the Cultural Revolution – beatings, public humiliation, mental and physical torture and even murder – Dai Ailian's fate was not as bad. But as well as the mental and physical deprivation she was forced to endure, it must have been particularly difficult for her to see all her years of hard work, helping to build a Chinese Ballet Company, now being mindlessly destroyed by one arrogant, power-crazed woman. In all the many conversations I have had with Dai Ailian, the only time I have seen this wise, warm, dignified and utterly humane woman lose her composure has been at the mere mention of Madame Mao's name.

But Dai Ailian is nothing if not a survivor. Her sense of humour shone through many of her stories of those difficult days of exile in the countryside. She happily relates a story about her loud snoring, which used to keep her dormitory companions awake at night. In desperation, they tied a rope to the foot of her bed, using it to rattle the bed and shake Dai awake when her snoring became unbearable. Finally, Dai and a fellow-snorer were banished to a large cupboard at night, where they were told they could snore to their heart's content, leaving their comrades to sleep in peace. 'On our first night in that cupboard,' Dai told me 'I tried to keep awake so as to hear the other snorer, in order to be able to experience what our dormitory companions had been complaining about.'

Among the women who were sent to work in the countryside in the same group as Dai Ailian, there was one of the joint choreographers of

The Red Detachment of Women, Jiang Zuhui. When I was in Beijing in May 2005, Jiang Zuhui spoke to me with great passion, recalling her time together with Dai during the Cultural Revolution. 'I want to tell you about this great lady,' she said 'about what a warm-hearted, selfless human being she is; and what a noble character she has. She never considered herself to be above anyone else. She could communicate as easily with the poorest, uneducated peasant as with the cleverest academic or the highest government official. During some of the most arduous periods of our banishment she never complained, nor did she ever try to pull rank in any way. "There's work to be done," she would say "and someone has to do it; so why not us?" '

'The more the guards tried to humiliate us, the less notice she took of them. When we were sent to the orchard to pick fruit Dai, being so short, couldn't reach the high branches; so she would concentrate on picking up the fruit that had fallen. The guards accused her of being lazy – even though, for a woman of her age, bending down to gather up the fallen fruit was actually much harder work than plucking it from the branches. When we tried to point out to the guards that Dai was not in very good health, their response was: "She looks sprightly enough cycling into the village." Every week we had to attend self-criticism meetings. A few people would try to use these sessions to ingratiate themselves with the guards by criticizing one of their peers. Occasionally someone would point a finger at Dai, saying falsely that she was not a dedicated worker. But she always retained her dignity and composure.'

By the mid-1970s the authorities were beginning to curb some of the most extreme aspects of the Cultural Revolution. A number of people, including Dai Ailian, were now 'half-liberated', meaning that their long period of hard labour in the countryside was being brought to an end and that they were given permission to return to the city. For Dai the most pressing problem was now the need to find somewhere to live (her previous accommodation having been confiscated by the government when they exiled her from Beijing). For the next few months, she was obliged to lead something of a vagabond existence, sleeping wherever she could find a bed for the night, with friends or former students.

In fact, it was one of Dai Ailian's original students from Chongqing, Wu Yi, who had been instrumental in persuading the authorities to allow her old teacher to return to Beijing. 'Dai had broken her arm and was in considerable pain, unable even to comb her hair,' I was told by Wang Kefen. 'So Wu Yi begged the guards to release Dai: ' you must let her return to Beijing. She's a National Treasure.' 'No, she's suspected of being a spy,' the guards said. 'I insist,' said Wu Yi, 'I'm taking her home. Here's my address. You can find her there if you need to.'

Wang Kefen, who was also originally a student of Dai Ailian's during her time in Shanghai, went on to describe how she went to visit Dai in the tiny room Wu Yi and Dai were sharing, now that Wu Yi had managed to get her old teacher back to Beijing. 'Isn't this fun,' said Dai, 'it's just like being in a train compartment!' 'She thanked me for visiting her and bringing her some fruit, but advised me not to come back again because, as my own husband had once been denounced as a "rightist", and as Dai was still suspected of being a spy, she felt that it might put me in danger if I were seen to be consorting with her.'

In 1975, Dai Ailian was ordered to start work again in the ballet department of the Beijing Dance School. This new assignment involved coaching some of the ballet teachers. Many of them had become listless and despondent after the years of inertia following Jiang Qing's systematic destruction of both the Dance School and the Ballet Company. Now, sadly, they failed to respond positively to Dai's attempts to raise the standard of their work. 'We know you are right,' they would say when Dai tried to correct some of the basic faults in their teaching, 'but we have become used to doing things this way and we can't change'. A deeply depressing state of affairs for someone whose approach to the teaching of classical ballet was as precise and meticulous as Dai Ailian's. This makes it all the more remarkable that, eventually – and partially thanks to the work of some of Dai's contacts in the West – the Beijing Dance School and the Central Ballet Company (now the National Ballet) were able not only to recover their former high standard of work but, in many respects, to surpass it.

By the end of 1976, Dai had finally found the apartment which was to become her permanent home and where I was to visit her many times between the winter of 2000 and the spring of 2005. Her living room there was dominated by a large painting of lotus blooms by the distinguished artist, Huang Yongfu. Dai told me that, one day, whilst he was putting the finishing touches to his painting (which covers almost the whole length of one wall in her living room), two of her other artist friends, Huang Miaozi and his wife, Yu Feng, arrived, both looking nervous and excited. They whispered something in Dai's ear. 'What was that,' she exclaimed, 'please say that again!' And she screamed with delight when they repeated that 'The Gang of Four have been arrested!' From that day, whenever Dai looked at Hong Yongfu's beautiful painting, it reminded her of that wonderful moment of liberation. Not just her own, but the liberation of the entire Chinese nation who, for ten long years, had been subjected to so much pain and useless destruction. 'We knew these terrible things couldn't last; but we did not know when they would end. Finally, that day had come.'

On hearing the good news Huang Yongfu, whose painting of a scene of lotus flowers was evocative of Dai Ailian's name – Lian meaning lotus flower in Mandarin – now added a white crane, the traditional bird-bearer of good fortune, to what was to become Dai's favourite painting. In the lower left-hand corner of the picture there is a calligrapher's elegant rendition of a highly symbolic Chinese poem. Roughly translated it reads: *After yesterday's wind and rain / The strong-feathered bird prepares to fly again / As the bright red colours of the lotus flowers / Rise once more above the pond's icy waters.*

Within weeks of the demise of the Gang of Four (they had not survived for long after Mao Zedong's death in September of 1976) Dai was starting to re-build her own life as well as that of the Ballet Company, now in her new capacity as the Company's Artistic Adviser. Having found out so much of what happened to Dai and to many of her associates during the Cultural Revolution, I began to wonder what life had been like for those ballet teachers and their students who had been in favour under Jiang Qing's regime? What had been their experience of that turbulent period in China's history?

The answer is to be found in Li Cunxin's eloquent autobiography, *Mao's Last Dancer.* (Penguin Books, Australia, 2003). In 1971, soon after Dai Ailian had been exiled to the countryside, the eleven-year-old Li Cunxin was plucked from a poverty-stricken family in rural north-east China to be trained at Madame Mao's newly 'sanitized' Dance Academy. He was undoubtedly selected not only for his physical aptitude, but also for his politically desirable peasant background. As well as ballet, Chinese folk dance and acrobatics, the training in the Beijing Dance School now also included a subject known as Madame Mao's Art Philosophy. This was intended to teach the students the importance of understanding that the arts were an essential political tool in China's on-going revolutionary struggle. Li Cunxin's autobiography gives a wonderfully vivid and detailed account of his evolution from a devoted disciple of Mao's communist ideals, via his gradual disillusion with Maoist propaganda, to his eventual defection to the West. His book is essential reading for anyone wanting to know exactly what was happening in the Beijing Dance School during the latter part of the Cultural Revolution, when so many fine artists were exiled to the countryside. This autobiography reveals how Madame Mao's actions were seen from the perspective of her fellow-travellers.

When Jiang Qing was eventually put on trial and later imprisoned, she claimed that in everything she did during the Cultural Revolution she was always acting on Mao's orders. 'I was his dog,' she insisted, 'and when he said bite I bit.' Dai Ailian was undoubtedly badly bitten by this evil woman; but, as we shall see, it was a bite from which she was determined to recover.

CHAPTER NINE

STARTING AGAIN

The last two decades of the twentieth century saw China's long, slow but inexorable process of recovery from the ravages of the Cultural Revolution, together with her gradual opening up to the West. Cultural exchanges began to be fostered with the USA, Canada, France and Britain and Dai Ailian was to play a major role in this process of cultural rapprochement. Inevitably, during the chaos of the Cultural Revolution, the standard of many of the dancers had seriously declined. Therefore, in order to rebuild the ballet company, a determined effort was made to revive works from the classical repertoire, such as *Swan Lake* and *Giselle*, which the Central Ballet had originally acquired from their guest Russian teachers in the late 1950s.

Thanks to Dai Ailian's sensitive coaching of several of the ballet company's young soloists and future principal dancers, it soon became possible for some of them to be entered in international ballet competitions. Outstanding among these were Mr Wang Cai Jun and Miss Wang Ci Feng who were coached by Dai for the first Paris International Ballet Concours in 1979 where they won the special prize awarded by the Paris Opera. Mr Wang Xin Hua and his partner, Xin Li Li of the Shanghai Ballet, also coached by Madame Dai, went on to win a series of awards at the second New York Ballet Competition, the Tokyo Asian-Pacific International Ballet Competition and, finally, the third International Paris Ballet Concours where they were awarded the Gold Medal. The dancers' standards of technical proficiency had by now clearly been re-established; but to what extent were the Chinese aware of the wider artistic developments in the West?

Anxious to acquaint herself with what had been happening in other parts of the world, Dai Ailian began paying regular visits to Europe and the USA, looking at the repertoires of various leading ballet companies, as well as searching for suitable guest teachers to invite to China. She soon renewed many of the contacts she had had in the 1930s with friends and colleagues in the London dance world, and she also began to make new contacts in Europe and America. The determination with which she now sought to widen the horizons of the Chinese ballet establishment and to raise the standard of the Central Ballet dancers was boundless. Yet her best efforts were all too often frustrated by entrenched

Dai Ailian circa 1986

attitudes among some bureaucrats concerning artistic policy decisions which were outside their professional, artistic, competence.

It is well to remind ourselves of the fact that in the arts, as is the case in all Chinese government-funded institutions, policy decisions were always strictly controlled by bureaucrats. If that is still largely the case today, it was certainly all the more so in the 1980s. A typical example of this occurred during the Central Ballet's first visit to the USA in 1986, when certain government officials travelling with the ballet company, ignoring Madame Dai's artistic judgement, proceeded to overrule some of her decisions concerning the casting of the repertoire, much to the detriment of some of the company's performances at the Washington DC Kennedy Centre. These were collective decisions initiated by officials, and Dai found herself out-voted. 'Later, at the airport, they admitted that they had been wrong to overrule my artistic decisions,' mused Dai Ailian with a wry smile and a philosophical shrug of the shoulders!

When she was free to travel to the West again, one of the first people whom Dai contacted was her original London ballet teacher, Anton Dolin, former star of Diaghilev's Ballets Russes and later one of the most important male dancers in the development of British ballet. When Dai first approached the Chinese authorities for permission to invite Anton Dolin to stage some of his productions for the Central Ballet, she was closely questioned about his age. He was already in his mid-seventies but, as Dai assured the relevant government officials, he was still in very good health. 'Well, in that case he can wait,' was the unenthusiastic reply. This was in the early 1980s, and China was still a little tentative concerning foreign guest artists. Needless to say, Dai persevered and, in 1983, she finally managed to obtain permission to invite Dolin to stage his charming version of the famous Romantic *Pas de Quatre* as well as his technically demanding male equivalent, the *Variations for Four* for the Central Ballet. The popular success of these two pieces led to an invitation for Dolin to allow the Central Ballet to acquire his exquisite version of *Giselle*. This was staged for the Company in 1984 by two of Dolin's protégés, Belinda Wright and Jelko Yuresha; it has remained one of the Company's most artistically satisfying productions.

Another important classical tradition which Dai was instrumental in introducing to China was that of the renowned Danish school of Bournonville. But perhaps the most important of the many foreign connections Dai Ailian was to make for the Chinese ballet was the one with Rudolf Nureyev, the charismatic male ballet star who had defected from Soviet Russia in a blaze of international publicity. He made a major

Celebrating Dai Ailian's 80th birthday, May 1996

contribution to the development of ballet in China and he and Dai Ailian also became firm friends.

It was on one of her visits to Paris that Dai was initially introduced to Rudolf Nureyev. That introduction was made by Ivor Guest, the doyen of British ballet historians, but also a greatly respected researcher into the history of the Paris Opera Ballet Company. (Interestingly, Ivor Guest is married to the Labanotation specialist, Ann Hutchinson, who had been at Dartington with Dai in the 1930s). Because it was through Ivor Guest that Dai Ailian was first introduced to the director of the Paris Opera (and later to Nureyev) many doors opened there for her, and consequently for ballet in China. This eventually led to Madame Dai being invited to be Guest Répétiteur with the artistic staff for the Paris Opera Ballet Company's production of *Don Quixote*, in 1986 at the Palais Garnier. In this performance the leading roles were performed by Miss Guo Pei Hui and Mr Zhao Ming Hua, two principal dancers from the Central Ballet.

When Dai Ailian was first introduced to Rudolf Nureyev, he immediately told her of his long-standing desire to visit China. Any such visit would have been difficult to arrange, not least because of Nureyev's indeterminate nationality status as a defector from Soviet Russia. Always realistic, Dai also pointed out to him that, financially, there was no way the Central Ballet would be able to afford to employ a star of his calibre.

Dai demonstrating a Chinese folk dance step during a dinner party. Beijing 2001

'But I don't want any money; I just want to experience working in China,' was Nureyev's disarming response. One would have thought that this was something the Chinese authorities should have welcomed; instead, they became suspicious of what they seemed to imagine was some sort of ulterior (possibly political) motive behind Nureyev's generous offer. What with one thing and another, it was to take some five years of scheming and persuading before it was finally possible for Nureyev's wish to visit China and to work with the Chinese dancers to be fulfilled.

For Nureyev's visit to China, the ballet Madame Dai invited him to stage was his own, much-admired production of *Don Quixote* because, unlike some other ballet classics, it is a work which offers a very wide range of good roles and technically demanding dancing for a large number of performers. Nureyev's staging of this ballet in Beijing was a remarkable success and, according to Dai Ailian, it represented one of the formative events in the development of ballet in China. It also sealed Nureyev's friendship with Dai. This had first blossomed in London at the time when Nureyev had shared a house with Maude and Nigel Gosling. Maude (née Lloyd) was an old friend of Dai's from her Rambert days in the 1930s. She and her husband, Nigel, had 'adopted' Rudolf Nureyev. Indeed, he used to refer to Maude as 'my English mother'. Now he declared that he had also acquired 'a Chinese mother' in Dai Ailian. (Sadly, due to his having defected from Soviet Russia, he had been cut off from his true, Russian mother).

I was struck by Dai's description of her first encounter with Nureyev: 'We didn't feel like two strangers, meeting for the first time. He insisted that he felt a special affinity with China.' 'I'm a Tartar,' he exclaimed 'and my father had been stationed in Harbin, in North East China.' Five years later, when Nureyev finally was able to come to China himself, Dai took him to see the famous Great Wall and teased him by saying that it had been built to keep the Tartars out! 'Ah, but now I'm on the inside' was his sly response.

Dai Ailian's achievements as an 'ambassador' for Chinese ballet are legion. It was she, informally, on private visits to Europe and America, as well as in her official capacity as Honorary Adviser to the Company, who undertook much of the publicity for the promotion of the Central Ballet prior to their initial visits to the USA, and later to London. As part of the Cultural Exchanges with the West, she was a guest teacher with the Washington Ballet and with the Fenice Opera Ballet in Venice. Another very important aspect of her efforts to cultivate a greater appreciation of China in the West, were the numerous lecture-demonstrations she gave all over the world on the rich heritage of Chinese folk dance. Interestingly, when lecturing in Canada or the USA, some of the audiences' questions related to the formative years of English ballet which Dai had witnessed at first hand in the 1930s.

Dai Ailian has sat on numerous committees and on the juries of several International Ballet Competitions, and she was honoured with a number of awards (see appendix). In addition to her pioneering work for both ballet and Chinese folk dance, she has made an important contribution to the Labanotation movement. Even in retirement, she has continued to promote China abroad and remained greatly respected and honoured by the Chinese government.

When I returned to teach in Beijing in the spring of 2005, I was also invited to attend Madame Dai's 89th birthday celebrations. This turned out to be nearly a week of partying, as the four main organisations founded by Dai Ailian each held a separate birthday celebration in her honour. The most elaborate of the four parties was the one given by the National Ballet of China and hosted by their Director, Madame Zhao Ruheng, in the Company's spacious studio theatre. Every single member of the Ballet Company had written his or her personal little birthday tribute to Dai. We were shown an excellent, specially prepared documentary film of her career, followed by a series of classical ballet divertissements performed by some of the Company's leading dancers. Then, a gigantic birthday cake was wheeled on and champagne was served, as a series of formal speeches were made in Dai's honour. But, for me, the most memorable and deeply moving moment was when I was quietly taken aside by one of the original choreographers of *The Red Detachment of Women* who, during the Cultural Revolution, had been exiled to the countryside together with Dai. With considerable emotion, she told me all about their shared experiences, and especially about Dai's fortitude and resilience during those terrible years. What a contrast with the present, assembled company of elegant young ballet dancers, none of whom had even been born during what the Chinese now refer to euphemistically as 'those difficult years'.

The next day, the Chinese Labanotation Society held a birthday tea party in Dai's apartment. These Laban ladies, some of them ballet teachers, others folk dance instructors, plus a few very earnest academics, had each brought along some sort of sweet or savoury speciality. This jolly occasion was the most 'homely' of Dai's four birthday parties and featured much happy reminiscing and posing for photographs; while the sheer diversity of these ladies' backgrounds, ranging as they did from a kindergarten teacher to a university professor, reflected the breadth of Dai Ailian's influence in the field of movement notation.

The next evening, the China Dancers Association hosted a lavish, formal banquet in Dai's honour at the Beijing Tibet Institute. Each of the amazing dishes served at this sumptuous feast apparently held some symbolic reference to longevity, good luck and prosperity. The party was attended by several important government officials, as well as by the Association's delegates from as far afield as Inner Mongolia and Urumqi. After the formal speeches and the seemingly endless presentation of gifts, everyone relaxed to enjoy the lively entertainment. Exquisitely costumed Tibetan girls sang and danced for us; a Korean minority dancer recited a poem; a Tibetan minstrel ended his serenade by presenting Dai with a long white scarf, a traditional Tibetan means of showing respect; a mysterious Mongolian song was followed by an exotic Uyghur dance. Finally, all of us, dancers, teachers and government officials, ended up joining hands in a Tibetan chain dance, led by Dai herself.

For me, the most memorable of all four birthday celebrations was the one hosted by the China Folk Song and Dance Ensemble. We gathered one morning in a rather spartan school hall and sat in small groups at round tables laden with bowls of pumpkin seeds, peanuts, sticky cakes and slices

Madame Dai Ailian, watching rehearsal of the National Ballet of China. This photograph was taken a few days before Dai Ailian's 89th birthday

of watermelon. As well as being in honour of Dai's birthday, this was also a celebration of the 90th birthday of Peng Song (who had worked with Dai, in the 1940s in Chongqing), as well as that of another nonegenarian, the artist Ding Tsung, one of the small group of friends who, together with Dai and her husband, had fled the Japanese invasion of Hong Kong. These 'three old dragons', as they were affectionately referred to in the welcoming speeches, were warmly embraced by former colleagues, few of them under the age of seventy, and some of whom had not seen each other in decades. As their womenfolk made these old men remove their flat caps and tidy their hair for the photographs, an exhausted Dai Ailian sat surrounded by a mountain of flowers and gifts, puffing away at a cigarette and reflecting on a Chinese dance experience spanning more than half a century.

Postscript

When I started researching this biography, a number of people wrote to me with personal reminiscences of Dai Ailian. The following are extracts quoted from their letters.

DAME BERYL GREY: A former prima ballerina with London's Royal Ballet Company, Dame Beryl was the Artistic Director of the London Festival Ballet Company from 1968 to 1979. She is also a past Chairman of the Imperial Society of Teachers of Dancing. The first British guest star to be invited to perform with the Central Ballet of China, she has recorded her reminiscences of that period in her book *Through the Bamboo Curtain*'(Collins, London, 1965).

'My very first meeting with Dai Ailian was in Beijing, in the spring of 1964. I had arrived there to dance with the Central Ballet Company. At that time Dai Ailian was the Director of the Ballet, as well as a Deputy to the People's Congress. Having been one of China's most famous dancers, Dai Ailian was highly regarded and respected. I found this tiny artist warm and welcoming, full of vitality and eager to learn, together with her company, all about ballet in the West.'

'Upon my return to Beijing with the Festival Ballet in 1979, I was appalled and saddened that she, her dancers and other artists, had been made to work in the fields during the Cultural Revolution. Yet, with indomitable spirit, she and the dancers were all trying hard to restore the Company and the art of ballet, despite those cruel years of deprivation so harmful to a dancer's body.'

'Dai Ailian is a courageous person, now much travelled internationally, retaining that friendly smile and vitality which mark her out as a most remarkable and valiant woman.'

SIR PETER WRIGHT: A soloist with the Sadler's Wells Theatre Ballet between 1949 and 1951, Peter Wright went on to a distinguished international career as ballet master and choreographer. He is the former Artistic Director of the Sadler's Wells Royal Ballet and the Birmingham Royal Ballet Companies, and is also a Governor of the Royal Ballet School and of Sadler's Wells Theatre.

'Among the many memories I have of Dai Ailian, two special ones stand out. The first was when the Sadler's Wells Royal Ballet was touring China in 1988 and she had been extremely helpful in advising us about the repertory that we should perform there. In Beijing, she invited some of us to her home. Not only did she provide excellent food, but she also showed us some marvellous films of the extensive research she was doing on the history of Chinese folk dance.'

'Ailian had also invited several people to meet us. This had been pretty difficult, as she was the only one who spoke both English and Chinese. She then showed us some folk dance steps and patterns and got us all to join in. She is a brilliant teacher and suddenly we were all dancing together, and the language barrier had been broken. What had started as a rather difficult evening ended up a triumph!'

'The other occasion I remember so well was when my wife and I, together with the eminent dance critic, Clement Crisp, were guests at a dinner party given by the Chinese ambassador to London. Dai Ailian was also present and, after dinner, Clement managed to persuade her to show us her version of the Chinese dance from *The Nutcracker.* It was truly delightful, and deliciously musical and she moved with such elegance, twirling a parasol in intricate gyrations around her head in a very charming and sensual manner. It was such a success that we begged for an encore!'

MONICA MASON: Following a long and distinguished career as a Principal Dancer with London's Royal Ballet, Monica Mason was appointed as the company's Principal Répétiteur in 1984. She has been the Director of the Royal Ballet Company since December of 2002.

'Madame Dai has had the most extraordinary life and I am so pleased to have known her. She has continued right up to the present day to be passionate about dance and her curiosity and energy made every moment spent with her stimulating, fascinating and rewarding. I admire her greatly and am thankful for her friendship.'

CHAPTER TEN

BALLET IN CHINA TODAY

At the time of writing, in the winter of 2005, there were six ballet companies in China: they were in Beijing, Shanghai, Guangzhou, Tianjin, Liaoning and Hong Kong. On the 24th of December 2000, five of these companies (the exception being the Hong Kong Ballet) joined forces for the first time to present a memorable gala performance in Beijing's Great Hall of the People. All five companies collaborated in a performance of Act Two of *Swan Lake*, while excerpts from a variety of ballets based on Chinese themes demonstrated something of the breadth of work created in China since the foundation of the Central Ballet in 1959.

The National Ballet of China: Founded in 1959, and originally known as the Central Ballet, this is the oldest, the largest and the most important Chinese ballet company. Madame Zhao Ruheng, formerly a dancer with the Central Ballet, has directed the National Ballet since 1994. The Company is based in Beijing and all the dancers are graduates of the Dance School of the Beijing Dance Academy. They include a number of world class artists, several of whom have been awarded medals at a number of major international ballet competitions.

In recent years, the National Ballet Company has undertaken several successful tours to Europe, the USA and throughout Asia, as well as performing in a number of Chinese cities. In addition to dancing most of the major classical repertoire, the National Ballet is committed to the creation of ballets based on Chinese culture and incorporating Chinese Classical and folk dance material. One of the Company's most successful Chinese ballets has been *Raise The Red Lantern*, a ballet version of Zhang Yimou's famous film of that name.

Several years of artistic isolation have now been replaced by the steadily increasing acquisition of works from the international repertoire. These have included Balanchine's *Serenade*, van Dantzig's *Four Last Songs* and Macmillan's *Concerto*.

The Shanghai Ballet: In 1966, a group of dancers from the Shanghai Dance School staged a performance of a new ballet, *The White Haired Girl* , which was to become as iconic a revolutionary work as was Beijing's Central Ballet's *The Red Detachment of Women.* In 1979, the

Han Po and Wang Qi Min in Act II of *Giselle* with the National Ballet of China

Women of the National Ballet of China in class

Hou Honglan and Meng Ningning in 'Raise the Red Lantern' – National Ballet of China

Wang Caijun (on the right), the Company's Ballet Master, with Shao Yaoguo, in Act I of 'The Red Detachment of Women' – National Ballet of China

Zhang Jian in 'The New Year Sacrifice' – National Ballet of China

troupe who had gained great popularity through their production of *The White Haired Girl* were officially re-constituted as the Shanghai Ballet Company. Although still attaching great importance to the staging of works based on Chinese themes, such as their full-length dramatic ballet *The Butterfly Lovers*, the Shanghai Ballet, under the direction of Xin Lili and Ha Muti, now has a considerable repertoire of major classical ballets. Recent foreign guest producers have included Pierre Lacotte, who staged the Paris Opera version of *Coppélia* and Derek Deane (former director of the English National Ballet) who mounted his version of *Romeo and Juliet* for the company. The Shanghai Ballet has toured successfully, both abroad and in China, and several of their young dancers have gained honours in international ballet competitions.

The Liaoning Ballet: Based in Shenyang, in the heavily industrialised north-east province of Liaoning, this is China's third-oldest ballet company (after Beijing's Central Ballet and the Shanghai Ballet). Founded in 1980, at a time when China was beginning to open up to the West, the Liaoning Ballet has built up a considerable international repertoire. However, some of its most popular productions have been works with indigenous themes, such as the much-acclaimed *The Moon Reflected in the Second Spring* and *Liang Shanbo and Zhu Yingtai*, which is

Zhang Jian in 'Raise the Red Lantern' – National Ballet of China

generally regarded as the Chinese *Romeo and Juliet*. With the rapid expansion of China, the Liaoning Ballet, directed by Wang Xun Yi, is able to provide an additional source of employment for the increasing number of professionally trained dancers now found throughout this vast country.

The Tianjin Ballet: Founded in 1992, the Tianjin Ballet is affiliated to the much older Song and Dance Theatre of Tianjin which dates back to 1959. The director, Liu Ying, has tended to favour Russian guest choreographers who have staged a version of *Spartacus* for the Company, as well as *Swan Lake* and the oriental fantasy ballet, *A Thousand and One Nights*. The Company consists of a core of professionally trained dancers, supplemented with dancers from folk dance ensembles, plus graduates from China's increasing number of private dance schools.

One of the Tianjin Ballet's recent successes has been a ballet inspired by the famous Chinese legend, *Jingwei Filling The Sea*. It tells the story of the daughter of an ancient emperor who drowned in the sea. Her spirit is transformed into a bird which flies back and forth, dropping pebbles into the water in an attempt to fill up the entire ocean.

The Guangzhou Ballet: Founded in 1996, the Guangzhou Ballet is China's youngest and fastest growing ballet company. Under the artistic direction of a former prima ballerina of the National Ballet, Zhang Dandan, this company has been attracting dancers from other Chinese companies and from the Beijing Dance Academy. It will now also be able increasingly to employ graduates from its own ballet school.

Maintaining a close rapport both with the National Ballet and with her contacts abroad, Zhang Dandan has established a wide-ranging repertoire. This includes ballets based on Chinese themes, such as *Xuan Feng* or *The Celestial Phoenix*; works by contemporary guest choreo-graphers, such as Prokovsky's *Anna Karenina* and versions of popular classics like *Coppélia* and *The Nutcracker*.

The Hong Kong Ballet: Under the direction of Stephen Jeffries (assisted by ballet mistress Rashna Homji) the long-established Hong Kong Ballet has developed into a successful ensemble, described by Clement Crisp of London's *Financial Times* as '... an enthusiastic company, as vital and inspiring as its city'.

In recent years, the Company's links with mainland China have been steadily strengthened, both by the participation of guest artists from

Beijing, and in particular through having acquired as its assistant director one of China's finest teachers, Wang Jia Hong. As one of the first graduates of the Beijing Dance School, way back in 1960, Mr Wang's presence in Hong Kong has established an important symbolic link with the earliest history of ballet in China.

As is the case with all Chinese ballet companies, the Hong Kong Ballet's repertoire includes a mixture of classical and modern works, many of the latter inspired by Chinese or other Asian themes. Two of these, Natalie Weir's *Turandot* and Wayne Eagling's *The Last Emperor* were successfully presented by the Company when they performed in Spain, in Madrid and at the 2005 Santander Festival.

The Beijing Secondary Dance School
The majority of the best professional dancers in China are graduates of Beijing's Secondary Dance School. Founded on the 6th of September 1954, the Dance School is now attached to the Beijing Dance Academy, regulated by the Ministry of Culture. The Dance School comprises four faculties: there is a seven-year ballet course and a six-year Chinese dance course, as well as four-year ballroom dance and four-year song and dance courses. All students receive some basic training in most subjects in addition to their own speciality.

In 2005, the Beijng Secondary Dance School had a total of 900 students, of which 300 were enrolled on the ballet course, starting at the age of ten or eleven, with almost equal numbers of boys and girls. In addition to their comprehensive vocational ballet training, their seven-year course included classes in Chinese folk dance, Chinese classical dance and some European national dance, as well as the normal secondary education programme.

Because they are selected from auditions held throughout China, the students are boarders at the Dance School. Nowadays, tuition and boarding are no longer free (as indeed they were in the past) but the fees are quite reasonable, and some scholarships are available for very talented students whose parents cannot afford to pay.

CHAPTER ELEVEN

THE PROBLEMS OF CHOREOGRAPHY IN CHINA

Although many Chinese dancers, and especially those in the National Ballet Company, are now of a standard comparable to the best in the world, the development of good choreography in China has been much less in evidence. The reasons for this are partly historical and partly cultural; nor can one overlook the role played by politics in this field. Before examining the various aspects of this problem in more detail, it would probably be useful, first of all, to consider what the term 'good choreography' implies.

Chambers dictionary definition of choreography is 'the art of arranging dances, especially ballets'. In the sense that this involves the selection and adaptation of steps from the vocabulary of the ballet classroom, fitting those movements to music, and devising suitable patterns and groupings, then most good dancers are perfectly capable of arranging dances. But good choreography is something both more complex and more subtle than mere dance arrangement. True choreography involves creating a sequence of movement images, combining dance, gesture and music in a coherent, organic whole. This may take the form of a narrative, or it may simply evoke a series of moods.

A truly inventive choreographer, responding sensitively to musical and visual stimuli, will be able to invent an individual way of moving, selecting, timing and re-moulding a step or a gesture so as to arouse the engagement and the emotion of the spectator. Such creative choreography transcends mere dance arrangement. The choreographer wanting to create a narrative ballet will also need to understand the principles of dramatic composition, as regards establishing the identity of each character, setting each scene and telling the story clearly and logically. Yet something which in a play may take a page of dialogue to convey can be reduced, in a ballet, to one telling gesture, or to a subtle movement phrase.

In the years immediately preceding the founding of the Central Ballet Company, Dai Ailian had choreographed a number of works for small dance groups in Sichuan province and later in Shanghai. Some of these dances were based on Chinese folk material; others were inspired by topical incidents relating to the desperate conditions in her war-torn homeland. The latter were no doubt influenced to some extent by Dai's admiration for the work of Kurt Jooss, while the former were the precursors of future Chinese dance theatre. An important factor in Dai's sensitive understanding of the art of choreography had, of course, been her exposure to the dynamic choreographic experiments taking place in Europe in the 1930s.

With the establishment of vocational ballet training in China and the subsequent founding of the Central Ballet Company, the future development of Chinese ballet was determined by guest teachers from Soviet Russia. From the point of view of the teaching of ballet technique and, later, the staging of works from the classical repertoire, the Russian influence was undoubtedly enormously valuable. Unfortunately, that was not the case as far as the development of creative choreography was concerned.

Some people maintain that choreography cannot be taught and that choreographers are born, not made. This is true to the extent that real creativity is something inborn; but there is also a whole area of practical craftsmanship which needs to underpin that creativity, and there are elements of that craftsmanship which can indeed be studied. In China, that task was undertaken by Pyotr Gusev. Naturally, his classes in choreography followed the Soviet Russian model. His classes were more in the nature of lessons in the craft of the dramatic staging of a dance work than in the creative art of choreography as this is understood in the West.

It is interesting to compare and contrast the development of ballet, and in particular that of choreography, in two countries which, prior to the early 1950s, had no indigenous ballet tradition. As we have seen, China was one such country; another was Turkey. Shortly after the end of the Second World War, at almost the same time as Soviet Russian teachers, led by Pyotr Gusev from St Petersburg, were establishing a vocational ballet school in Beijing, a number of British ballet teachers were setting up the first Turkish State Ballet school in Istanbul (and later in Ankara) under the supervision of Dame Ninette de Valois, the director of London's Royal Ballet.

By the 1960s, both the Chinese and the Turkish ballet schools had trained a sufficient number of good dancers to make it possible to stage classical ballets such as *Swan Lake* and *Giselle*. However, in terms of new choreography, the Chinese (coached by Gusev) were closely following the Soviet model. This favoured narrative ballets, structured to a set, dramatic formula; whereas the Turks (guided by de Valois) were benefitting from an approach to choreography which placed greater value on the individual, creative freedom associated with the arts in the

West. During the decade spanning the mid-1960s to the mid-1970s, while the Turks were therefore acquiring an artistically varied repertoire, the Chinese Cultural Revolution was rejecting foreign influences and, more importantly, the concept of individual, artistic creativity. Such artistic endeavour as still existed in China was now strictly limited by the requirement to conform to the Communist government's ideological dictates. Any new work had to be created collectively, by a group of artists.

With the gradual 'opening up' of China from around the 1980s, ballet in that country became increasingly receptive to a variety of foreign influences, but was still able to retain many of its own, indigenous characteristics. Nowadays, many Western dance companies visit China regularly, and the Chinese National Ballet Company has undertaken a number of successful overseas tours. Yet, in spite of some serious efforts to stimulate the development of interesting new choreography, why has that area remained the weak link in the development of ballet in China?

Choreographers don't grow on trees. Nor can true choreography really be taught(although some grounding in the craft of dance composition can be a useful tool in the nurturing of choreographic talent). What is needed is for young artists to be given the space to experiment; both the emotional space and, in practical terms, studio space and willing, co-operative dancers. When I was a guest teacher at the Beijing Dance School in the winter of 2001, my past experience in directing the dance composition course at London's Royal Ballet School prompted me to try to persuade the Chinese to start something along similar lines. However, in those days, the sort of individual, expressive freedom inherent in such a course would not have sat comfortably on the then still very rigid nature of Chinese society.

On a more recent visit to Beijing (in the spring of 2005) I was able to discuss with the Director of the National Ballet, Madame Zhao Ruheng, the on-going problem of nurturing new choreographic talent in China. I was heartened to hear of recent plans to establish choreographic workshops as part of the curriculum at the Beijing Dance Academy. I was also interested to know how Madame Zhao saw the future of the Company developing and, in particular, whether there were any signs of interesting young Chinese choreographers emerging? She named two young dancers showing some promise in that direction: Fei Po and Wang Juan Yuan.

As to Zhao Ruheng's vision of the future, her ambition is to see the development of new work which combines classical ballet schooling with authentic Chinese dance and some elements of modern dance. If this synthesis can be successfully achieved – and in the new China everything seems possible – that will also go a long way towards fulfilling Dai Ailian's original vision of the future of dance in China. Whether Dai's own concept of subtle, artistically sensitive choreography (nurtured as it was in the cosmopolitan, creative environment of Western Europe in the mid-1930s) could ever really take root in China remains to be seen. The Chinese people's natural love for bold, large-scale spectacle remains at odds with that concept. Yet, in a huge country like China, with such a diverse population, there may well be room for both.

CHAPTER TWELVE

CLASS WITH THE CHINESE BALLET

In December of 2000, I was first invited to teach for one month at the Dance School which feeds the National Ballet Company of China. I taught the sixteen-year-old boys and the twelve-year-old girls, and I was enormously impressed by the very high standard of all the students I encountered. Although I did see one performance given by the company, I did not get the opportunity at that time to see a company class. When, three years later, that company gave a series of performances at London's Sadler's Wells Theatre, I wanted to see if any of the young men I had taught in Beijing were now members of the company. Waiting at the stage door, I soon came across Wang Hao, the one student in my class who spoke a little English. Now it was my turn to try out my few, newly-acquired phrases of Mandarin on him. This generated much excitement, and I was soon surrounded by no fewer than five of the boys who had been in my classes in Beijing and who were now in the National Ballet Company. They were on their way to their daily company class, and they invited me to accompany them. What a treat this turned out to be.

During my time at the Beijing Dance School I had witnessed the fine teaching of the ballet faculty under the direction of Mr Cao (the father of the Birmingham Royal Ballet's principal dancer, Ci Cao), so I was certainly expecting a high standard; but the class I was about to see exceeded even my very high expectations. The sheer dynamic energy of ballet master Wang Cai Jun's teaching was thrilling to witness, as were his elegantly crafted, beautifully musical enchainements. His teaching was clearly informed by the best elements of the Russian school, which underpins ballet training in China; but the Chinese have have put their own, distinctive stamp on this. Their rendering of the *danse d'école* had a clarity and a freshness totally devoid of any of the mannerisms one sees in some Russian dancers, and particularly in their Western imitators.

The first thing that struck me was the pace of Wang Cai Jun's class. There was none of that endless, self-indulgent hanging about at the barre, now all too common in the West. In less than twenty-five minutes he had put the dancers through a perfectly judged series of barre exercises. Although every single dancer in the company (men as well as women) can get their legs way up past their ears, they knew when this was appropriate and when an exercise called for a 45 degree angle with a more subtle use of lower-leg work. What a pleasure it was to see these dancers treating class as a serious training session rather than as the cautious warm-up it sometimes turns into. In the centre, after several demanding adagio enchainements which everyone tackled with admirable determination and aplomb, I counted no less than eight challenging allegro combinations.

About half of the allegro enchainements were performed by both the women and the men, with no concessions regarding speed made for the male dancers. Some of them were very tall indeed, but six-foot-something Hao Bin and Hu Da Yong, with his mile-long legs, sprinted through the fastest of steps with the greatest of ease. Then came the men's big, slow jumps, interspersed with brilliant pirouettes and tours, all danced with a delightful combination of skill and obvious enjoyment. I was a little less impressed with the young women in the corps de ballet. Beautiful, loose-limbed and elegant as they all were, there was something slightly bland about their dancing. Was this perhaps to do with natural, Chinese feminine restraint? Or was it, as I rather suspected, that they had for too long been fed on a dance diet of swans and sylphs? But one thing was certain: all these young men and women had a superb example in the meticulous demonstration of their still very active teacher. It was clear that Wang Cai Jun had himself been a splendid dancer.

When I returned to teach in Beijing in the spring of 2005, I had the opportunity of meeting Wang Cai Jun again. He told me a fascinating story which explained why his work is so delightfully musical. In 1979, Dai Ailian was coaching the young Cai Jun for his participation in the Paris International Ballet Competition. With only days to go, he sustained an injury which called for a week's complete rest. Madame Dai, determined that no precious rehearsal time should be lost, provided her young dancer with a recording of the music for his competition dances, ordering him to lie down and spend several hours a day listening to the music and breathing with it while visualising each dance step rhythmically. 'That experience was the turning point in my career', said Wang Cai Jun.

During my 2005 visit to Beijing, I was able to see something of the work of two other excellent Chinese ballet masters who happened to be guest-teaching with the National Ballet Company. Both men had also worked extensively outside of China, broadening the scope of their original Soviet Russian-based schooling. It was a pleasure to see Mr Zhao Ming Hua's beautifully modulated, rhythmically precise exercises in the men's class. He re-introduced two movements not much favoured by the

Wu Jingshu (Lollie), Madame Dai's assistant and interpreter, with the author, Beijing 2001

Soviets but which are fundamental to classical training in the West: the Cecchetti type of frappé, so essential for developing fast footwork, and the chassé using a sliding action of the sole of the foot along the floor, giving a particular texture to this movement much favoured by teachers and choreographers outside of Russia.

The other Chinese guest teacher whose class I was invited to observe at that time, Mr Wang Jiahong, has taught both at London's Royal Ballet School and in Australia and, at the time of writing, he was ballet master and assistant director of the Hong Kong Ballet (of which Stephen Jeffries was still the director). His class managed to combine some of the best features of both Russian and Western classical schooling; his use of rapid changes of weight, together with the lightning speed of his footwork and his deliciously playful use of épaulement kept the girls' class alive with energy.

One of the most valuable legacies of the Soviet Russian involvement in China has been the superb teaching of partnering skills the Chinese acquired from Sebrenikov. Wang Jiahong has excelled in this area and, as guest pas de deux teacher on frequent visits to London's Royal Ballet School, he has made a major contribution to the teaching of this subject in Britain. Both he and his wife, Tang Xiuyun (who has also taught extensively in China and abroad) graduated from the Beijing Dance School in 1960. Having been trained by the Russians, they also worked closely with Dai Ailian during the early 1960s. Both of them are therefore fine examples of the direct link from the earliest days of ballet in China to the present day. Not only has that link managed to survive the difficulties of the Cultural Revolution, but it has also gone on both to absorb from and to contribute to ballet in the West.

A CHRONOLOGICAL OVERVIEW OF
DAI AILIAN'S CAREER

Dancer
Teacher and Coach for Classical Ballet and Chinese Dance
Choreographer
Researcher in Chinese Dance History
Chinese Dance Lecturer and Demonstrator

BACKGROUND
Born in Trinidad of Cantonese parents on 10th May 1916. Educated at
St. Hilary's High School, Port of Spain. Studied ballet from the age of
eight with Nell Walton. Started teaching ballet before moving to London
in 1931. She lived in England until 1940, studying ballet with Dolin,
Rambert and Craske.

Choreographed and performed dances for fund-raising concerts held in
aid of Chinese victims of Sino-Japanese war. Studied modern dance in
London with several teachers before being awarded a scholarship to study
with Jooss at Dartington. Moved to China in 1940 to research Chinese
dance history as well as the folk dances of many of China's Ethnic
Minority Populations.

CHOREOGRAPHY AND PERFORMANCE
In London:

1935	*Beggar*. Chinese dance (Solo)
1935	*March*. Chinese dance (Solo)
1936	*Weeping Willows*. Chinese dance (Solo)
	The Concubine dances for the Emperor (Solo)
1939	*Alarm*. Chinese dance (Solo)

In Hong Kong:

1940	*Ruth the Gleaner*. Biblical dance (Solo)
	East River. Chinese dance (Solo).

In Chongqing, Sichuan:

1941	*Longing for Home*. Chinese neo-classical dance (Solo)

1942	*Sale.* Chinese contemporary dance (Short ballet)
1943	*Moon of the Miaos.* Chinese Dance (Pas de deux)
	Dances of Youth. Uyghur folk dances (Solo, Duet, Quartet)
	Air Raid. Chinese dance (Short ballet)
	Dream. Modern dance (Pas de deux)
	Guerilla Coup. (Short ballet)
1944	Yao Ceremonial Dance. Chinese dance (Solo, Trio)
	The Mute and the Cripple. Chinese classical dance. (new version, 1950, *Lao Bei Xiao*)
	Auntie Zhu Presents Eggs to the Army (Yang-ge. Short ballet)
	Mme. Kan Ba Han. Uyghur folk dance (Pas de deux)
1946	*Happy Cocks.* Kanba Tibetan folk dance (Group)
	Tibetan Spring. Kanba Tibetan folk dance (Group)
	Lolo Love Song. (Group dance)
1943-1946	Many performances of most of the above in Guilin, Guizhou, Chengdu and Chongqing.
1946	Four solo performances in Yi Yuan, Shanghai.

In Beijing:

1949	*Victory of the Chinese People.* Collective choreography (Panorama)
1950	*Construction of the Motherland.* Yang-ge
	Doves of Peace. neo-classical ballet (Principal dancer)
1953	*Lotus Dance.* neo-classical Chinese dance (Group)
1955	*Flying Apsaras.* neo-classical Chinese dance (Duet)
1961	*Heroic Little Eighth Routers.* Short Chinese ballet for children
1954-1955	Toured India, Burma and Indonesia, studying and performing dances of those countries as Artistic Director of Chinese Cultural Delegation.

PROFESSIONAL POSITIONS AND TEACHING

1942-1943	Dance teacher, Chongqing National Opera School
1943-1944	Dance teacher, National Social Education Institute, Chongqing
1944-1947	Head of Dance Section of the Yu Cai School, Chongqing
1947-1948	Teacher and Principal, Shanghai Music and Dance Academy
1948-1949	Professor of Dance, Peiping Art Academy, Beijing
	Professor of Dance, Peiping Teachers College Beijing

1949-1950 Head of Dance Section (Arts Dept.) North China University
1950-1955 Head of Dance, Central Folk Song and Dance Ensemble
1954-1964 Principal of the Beijing Dance School
1963-1966 Artistic Director, Central Ballet of China (now the National Ballet)
1976-2006 Artistic Adviser to the Central Ballet of China.

Besides teaching in China, Dai Ailian has been Guest Teacher in the USA with the Washington Ballet, in Italy with the Ballet of the Fenice Opera, and Guest Repetiteur at the Paris Opera in 1986 for the performance of *Don Quixote* with Guest Principal Dancers from the Central Ballet of China.

JUROR OF COMPETITIONS
Juror at International Ballet Competitions in Paris, New York, Jackson, Tokyo, Turin and Shanghai and at Folk Dance Competitions at Youth Festivals in Bucharest and Moscow

SOCIETIES

1949-1954 President, China Dancers Association
1954-1984 Vice-President, China Dancers Association
1984-   Honorary President China Dancers Association
1980-1981 Executive Member, Conseil International de la Danse (CIDD), UNESCO, Paris.
1981-1985 Vice-President, CIDD, UNESCO, Paris
1982-   President, China National Committee, CIDD
           Chairman, Labanotation Society of China Dancers Assoc.
           Chairman, China Ballet Society of China Dancers Assoc.
1979-   Member of International Council, Kinetographie Laban and Labanotation, UK-USA
1991-   Board Member, World Presidents of Folk Arts International UNESCO (Austria)

RESEARCHER AND LECTURER
Researched extensively in the remote mountains of South West China, collecting the dances of many of the Ethnic Minority Peoples and recording some of these in Labanotation. Has lectured on the history of Chinese dance and has given numerous demonstrations of Chinese folk dance throughout the world.

PRIZES AND RECOGNITION

1950   Model Worker as Principal Dancer and Choreographer for the ballet *Doves of Peace*

1951   Third Prize, choreography *Tibetan Spring*, Youth Festival, Berlin

1953   Second Prize, choreography *Lotus Dance* Youth Fest. Bucharest

1955   Third Prize, choreography *Flying Apsaras* Youth Festival, Warsaw

1995   Winner of the 20th Century Choreographic Award in Beijing for her contribution to Chinese choreography.
Patron, Dance Notation Institute, University of Surrey
Patron, Language of Dance Centre, London
First Grade Artist, Peoples Republic of China
Honorary Member, Federation of Writers and Artists Union
Fellow of the Hong Kong Academy of Performing Arts
Honorary Member, Beijing International Society
Honorary Member, Cecchetti Society and Cecchetti International

Dai Ailian is the author of *Chinese Dance* Microsoft Encarta Encyclopaedia de luxe 99 cd Set: XO3

Index

References to illustrations are given in italics.

Artists International, 10, 19
Ashton, Frederick, 7

Bai Shuxiang, 48
Balanchine, George, 7
ballets and other choreography, see
    also Dai Ailian, choreography;
    Tibetans; Yao people; Yi people
  Anna Karenina, 87
  Bluebells in Fairyland, 2
  Butterfly Lovers, The, 85
  Concerto, 82
  Coppélia, 85, 87
  Corsaire, Le, 49
  Don Quixote, 74–75
  Duan Gung, 29
  fille mal gardée, La, 49
  Fountain of Tears, The, 50
  Four Last Songs , 82
  Giselle, 49, 73, 83
  Green Table, The, 12–13, 27
  Jingwei Filling the Sea, 87
  Last Emperor, The, 88
  Liang Shanbo and Zhu Yingtai, 85
  Maid of the Sea, The, 49
  Moon Reflected in the Second Spring,
    The, 85
  New Year Sacrifice, The, 50, 85
  Notre Dame de Paris, 50
  Nutcracker, The, 63, 80, 87
  Pas de Quatre, 73
  Raise the Red Lantern, 82, 84, 86
  Red Detachment of Women, The, 51,
    52, 53, 64–65, 67, 82, 84
  Romeo and Juliet, 85
  Serenade, 82
  Spartacus, 87
  Swan Lake, 48–50, 82, 87
  Sylphides, Les, 8, 10, 32, 50
  Thousand and One Nights, A, 87
  Turandot, 88
  Variations for Four, 73
  White Haired Girl, The, 51, 64, 82,
    85
  Xuan Feng or The Celestial Phoenix,
    87
Ballets Jooss, 12–13
Ballets Russes, 7–8
Batang Xuanzi dances, 28
Beihai park, 39
Beijing, 39, 64, 82, see also Peiping
Beijing Dance Academy, 25, 45, 58,
    82, 87–88
Beijing Dance School, 45–49, 68–69,
    91
Beijing Opera, 62, 64–65
Beijing Secondary Dance School, 88,
    93
Beijing Tibet Institute, 77
Berk, Ernst and Lotte, 12
Bolshoi Ballet, 46
Bournonville style, 59, 73
Burrows-Goossens, Lesley, 11-12

Cao, Mr, 93
Cecchetti, Enrico, 8, 14, 46, 59
  method, 8, 46–48
Central Ballet of China, 47, 48, 50–
    51, 52, 62, 64–65, 68, 71, 73–74,
    76, 79, 89–90, see also National
    Ballet of China
Central Ballet School, 45
Central Drama Academy, 42
Central Folk Song and Dance
    Ensemble, 42, 45, 77
Central Philharmonic Orchestra, 62,
    64

Chappell, William, 7
Chen, Sylvia, 2
Chengdu, 21, 27, 32
Chiang Kaishek, 23, 38, 65
China Campaign Committee, 11, 19–20
China Defence League, 20
China Institute, 11, 19–20
Chinese Borderlands, 27, 29, 43
Chinese Civil War, 23, 38
Chinese classical dance, 45
Chinese Dance Theatre, 42
Chinese Dancers' Association, 54
Chinese folk dance, 32, 39, 42–43, 54–55, 58, 75, 76, 80
Chongqing, 21, 23–25, 27, 29, 32, 64
choreography in China, 49, 89–92
    pointe work, 42, 51, 53, 65
    classical ballet in China
    establishing, 44–53
    today, 82–88
Craske, Margaret, 8, 32, 47, 59
Crisp, Clement, 87
Cultural Revolution, 53, 61–70

Dai Ailian:
    birth, 2
    family, 1–2, 3, 4, 5, 10
    childhood, 1–6
    early experience of ballet, 2, 4
    moves to London, 4
    studies ballet in London, 7–12
    performs in *Hiawatha* at the Albert Hall, 7
    performing in London, 9
    early choreography, 10–11
    begins study of modern dance, 11
    studies at Dartington, 13–18
    sculpted portrait by Willi Soukop, 15, 16
    awareness of Chinese roots, 19
    in Hong Kong, 19–22
    marriage, 21
    undergoes surgery in Hong Kong, 23
    travels in China, 23–43
    flees Japanese invasion of Hong Kong, 24
    appointed head of dance and Yu Cai School, 27
    'Borderlands Music and Dance' performance, 29
    in New York, 34
    performing Peng Song's choreography, 35
    dances for People's Liberation Army, 39
    The Victory of the Chinese People pageant, 40
    gives a dance class to factory workers, 41
    as an icon of Chinese folk dance, 42
    on teaching, 47
    on Cecchetti, 59
    exile in the countryside, 65–66
    after the Cultural Revolution, 71–81
    a chronological overview, 96–99
    choreography:
    Air Raid, 25, 38
    Alarm, 37
    Doves of Peace, 41, 42
    Flying Apsaras, 42–43
    Lao Bei Xiao, 29, 31, 32
    Longing for Home, 25, 26
    Lotus Dance, 42
    Mute and the Cripple, The, 29
    Ruth the Gleaner, 33
    Sale, 25
    list of choreography and performance, 96–97
Dai Yao, 2, 4, 10, *see also* Dai Ailian, family
Dance Notation Bureau, 54
Dancing Times, 4
Danish Royal Ballet, 44, 59
Dartington, 13–19, 27, 39, 74

de Valois, Ninette, 7, 90
Deane, Derek, 85
Diaghilev, Serge, 7–8
Ding Tsung, 79
Dolin, Anton, 4, 6–7, 73
Du Ming Xin, 53
Dunhuang caves, 42

Elirov, Edouard, 44
Elmhirst, Leonard and Dorothy, 13
ethnic minority peoples, 27–29, 40,
    42–43, 59, 77, *see also* Jia Rong
    people; Khampas people;
    Mongolians; Quiang people;
    Tibetans; Yao people; Yi people

Fei Po, 91
Fenice Opera Ballet, 76
Folkwang Tanzbuhne, 13
Fonteyn, Margot, 44
Fox, Eileen, 54

Gang of Four, 53, 62, 64, 68–69
Goncharov, Georgi, 44
Gosling, Maude (née Lloyd), 7, 75
Gosling, Nigel, 75
Graham, Martha, 11
Great Leap Forward, 61
Grey, Beryl, 50–51, 79
Guangzhou, 21, 82
Guangzhou Ballet, 87
Guest, Ivor, 74
Guilin, 32
Guizhou, 32
Guo Pei Hui, 74
Gusev, Pytor, 46, 48–50, 90

Ha Muti, 85
Han majority, 40, 43
Han Po, *83*
Hao Bin, 94
Heckroth, Hein, 14, 16
Homji, Rashna, 87
Hong Kong, 19–24, 44, 82
Hong Kong Ballet, 82, 87–88, 95

Hou Honglan, *84*
Hu Da Yong, 94
Huang Miaozi, 68
Huang Yongfu, 68–69
Hutchinson, Ann, 74
Hyman, Prudence, 7

Imperial Russian Ballet, 8

Japanese invasion of China, *see*
    prologue
Jeffries, Stephen, 87
Jia Rong people, 29, *30*, *35*
Jiang Qing (Madame Mao), 53, 62–
    66, 68–70
Jiang Zuhui, 50, 53, 67
Jooss, Kurt, 12–14, 27, 90

Kahl, Dorothy, 10
Kahl, Peggy, 10
Khampas people, 27–28
Kirov Ballet, 46
Kumbarhan, 38
Kunqu opera, 40
Kuomintang, 23, 38, 40, 65

Laban, Rudolf von, 13–14, 54, 59
    space-movement theories of, 14,
    43
labanotation, 14, 54–60
    examples of, 56–57
Labanotation Society of China, 54,
    77
Lacotte, Pierre, 85
Leach, Bernard, 14
Leeder, Sigurd, 13–14
    technique, 39
Leisovich, Tamara, 46
Li Chen Xiang, 53
Li Cunxin, 69
Liaoning, 82
Liaoning Ballet, 85
Liu Qingtang, 48
Liu Ying, 87
Lloyd, Maude *see* Gosling, Maude

London Festival Ballet, 79
Long Zheng Qiu, 25, 34
Lu Xin, 42

Ma Si Chong, 25
Ma Yunhong, 50
Macmillan, Kenneth, 82
Mao Zedong, 23, 38–39, 49–51, 61,
    63–64, 69
Markova, Alicia, 4, 7
Mason, Elizabeth (Betty), 10, 12
Mason, Monica, 80
Mei Lang Feng, 38, 42
Meng Ningning, *84*
Ministry of Culture, 40
modern dance
    American, 11
    Central European, 13, 27
    German expressionist dance
    movement, 11
Mongolians, 40, 77
Moser, Simone, 16, 18

Nanjing, 40
National Ballet of China, 49, 76, 82,
    83–86, 91, 93, *see also* Central
    Ballet of China
National Institute for Social
    Education, 24
National Opera School, 24
Nijinsky, Vaslav, 8
North China University, 45
Nureyev, Rudolf, 73–76

Ouyang Yuqian, 40

Paris Opera Ballet, 74
Paris–Prague Peace Conference, 39–
    40
Pavlova, Anna, 8
Peiping, 32, *see also* Beijing
Peiping Art Academy, 39
Peiping Teachers College, 39
Peng Song, 24–25, 27–29, 34, *35*,
    39, 79

People's Liberation Army, 39
People's Republic, 39, 49, 51
'propaganda ballets', 51, 53

Quiang people, 28–29

Rambert, Marie, 7, 45, 47
Red Guards, 61, 64
Red Star Over China, 19
Royal Ballet School, 91, 95
Russian revolution, 44
Ryan, Mabel, 47

Sadler's Wells Ballet, 7, 44
Sadler's Wells Ballet School, 44
Sadler's Wells Royal Ballet, 80
Sadler's Wells Theatre Ballet, 80
Sebrenikov, Nicolai, 46, 48, 95
shamans, 29
Shangdong province, 39
Shanghai, 27, 32, 34, 38–40, 44, 82
Shanghai Ballet, 71, 82, 85
Shanghai Dance School, 51, 82
Shao Yaoguo, *84*
Shengli oil fields, 39
Shi Shenfang, 50
Shi Yi Qui, 20
Sichuan, 23, 27, 29
Sino-Japanese War, 19, 20, 25, 40
Snow, Edgar, 19
Sokolova, Lydia, 8, 32
Song and Dance Theatre of Tianjin,
    87
Soukop, Wilhelm Josef (Willi), 14, *15*,
    16, 18, 20, 21
Soviet Russian system of teaching,
    46–49, 59
Star, Kay, 14
Sukolsky, 39, 44
Sun Yat Sen, Madame (Song
    Quingling), 20–21

Tang Xiuyun, 95
Tao Xin Zhi, 27
Tiananmen Square, 39

Tianjin, 44, 82
Tianjin Ballet, 87
Tibetans, 40, 77
   Shounan Qinbu, 57–58
   traditional costume, *60*
Toropov, George, 44
Toye, Wendy, 7
Trinidad, 1–2
Tsaplin, Viktor, 46
Tudor, Antony, 7
Turkish State Ballet School, 90–91

Uyghur folk dancers, 38, 77
Uyghur people, 29, 40

Vaganova, Agrippina, 46
Volkova, Vera, 44

Walton, Nell, 1–2, 4
Wang Cai Jun, 71, 93–94
Wang Caijun, *84*
Wang Ci Feng, 71
Wang Hao, 93
Wang Hongwen, 64
Wang Jia Hong, 88, 95
Wang Juan Yuan, 91
Wang Ke Fen, 32, 34, 38, 67–68
Wang Qi Min, *83*
Wang Xin Hua, 71
Wang Xixian, 50, 53
Wang Xun Yi, 87
Wang Zu Qiang, 53
Washington Ballet, 76
Wigman, Mary, 11-12
Wolz, Carl, 54–55
Woodhouse, George, 10
Wright, Belinda, 73
Wright, Peter, 80
Wu Jingshu (Lollie), 54, *95*
Wu Yi, 34, 67–68

Xia Dynasty, 28
Xin Li Li, 71, 85
Xinjiang, 29, 38

Yangge, 43
Yangtze river, 23
Yao people, 40
   Ceremonial Dance, 36
Yao Wenyuan, 64
Ye Chien Yu, 21, *22*, 23, 32
   drawings by, *26*, *30–31*, *33*, *36–37*
Yen Ju Dui, 32
Yi people, 28–29
   Moon Dance, 55–56
Yu Cai School, 27
Yu Feng, 68
Yuresha, Jelko, 73

Zhang Chunqiao, 64
Zhang Dandan, 87
Zhang Jian, *85–86*
Zhang Su Li, 20
Zhang Yimou, 82
Zhao Ming Hua, 74, 94
Zhao Ruheng, 76, 82, 91
Zhou Dynasty, 28
Zhou Enlai, 21, 32, 48
Zorina, Vera, 7